Encouraging Yourself in the Most Holy Faith

Chris A. Legebow

ISBN-13: 978-0-9952715-9-3

DEDICATION

I thank God for the Macchiavello family especially the worship and praise ministry. Worshipping God is a mighty weapon. I thank God for Joyce Meyer, Kenneth and Gloria Copeland, Marilyn Hickey and Benny Hinn. I thank God for Trinity Broadcasting Network.

Truly Christian media has made a huge impact on my life. God has used these and other preachers to speak RHEMA words of God to me and encouraged me and strengthened me through linking together the Church of North America and the global Church also.

CONTENTS

ACKNOWLEDGMENTS

All Scripture taken from Biblegateway.com
Most Scripture Modern English Version (MEV)
Some Scripture King James Version (KJV)

1 THE ARMOUR OF GOD

Jude 1: 20 But you, beloved, build yourselves up in your most holy faith. Pray in the Holy Spirit. 21 Keep yourselves in the love of God while you are waiting for the mercy of our Lord Jesus Christ, which leads to eternal life.

22 On some have compassion, using discernment. 23 And others save with fear while pulling them out of the fire, hating even the garment stained by the flesh.

24 Now to Him who is able to keep you from falling and to present you blameless before the presence of His glory with rejoicing, 25 to the only wise God our Savior, be glory and majesty, dominion and power, both now and forever. Amen.

Before you can truly start encouraging yourself in the most Holy Faith, you must get properly dressed. The truth is the need for encouragement is proof that you are in a war. It is a war that is spiritual. You must put on Spiritual armour. Only God's Spirit can fight against what fights against you.

It is so special to be built up by others in the Christian Church. Christians with Christians can sharpen each other making them both more excellent. Often at Church Christians encourage each other. The pastor may speak a word that directly builds up and encourages you. There are occasions though when you must encourage yourself in God. Your spirit must rise up and take authority over your soul. You are a spirit; you have a soul and you live in a human body. If you have been born again, baptized in the Holy Spirit and are living a Christian life, you are always more than a conqueror over anything in your life. God has created you to live a victorious joyful life.

God is First

First, you must know how to build up yourself. You must feed your spirit. Only the Holy Spirit can feed the human spirit. Prayer and praise will get you focused on God; God's Holy Spirit will fill your human spirit will give you peace, joy, the fruit of the Spirit. Your focus on God, will take the focus off yourself.

It is essential that you build your relationship with God each day, not just in a day when you are overwhelmed. God's presence and communion with God will strengthen you and help you to see things from an eternal perspective. Praise and worship are excellent means of your love for God and His love for you. As you praise and worship God, His Holy Spirit, fills your human spirit. In His light, no darkness can stay. Living a lifestyle of prayer and praise and worship, will strengthen your inner man so that you are strong on the inside.

Praying in tongues and praising in tongues are ways to go beyond all earthly help. As you pray in the Holy Spirit and praise in the Holy Spirit, God is praying in you and through you the perfect will of God for you.

Romans 8: 26 Likewise, the Spirit helps us in our weaknesses, for we do not know what to pray for as we ought, but the Spirit Himself intercedes for us with groanings too deep for words. 27 He who searches the hearts knows what the mind of the Spirit is, because He intercedes for the saints according to the will of God.

If your situation is the direct result of sin, repent. Quickly go to your Saviour and plead the blood of Jesus over your life. Pray that God will show mercy towards you. God is merciful and if we confess our sins, He will forgive us. If your situation is the result of someone else's sin, plead the blood of Jesus over yourself and ask God for mercy for that person. If someone sins against you, God will fight against him or her. Even though you may not feel like praying for that person, pray mercy on the person that God may lead him or her to repentance.

Prayer

Begin to pray daily "Thank you God that you can keep me from falling". God not only forgives us, but can keep us living Holy. The empowering presence of the Holy Spirit can keep us living for God and hating sin. It's not merely positive thinking; it is Divine mercy and empowering presence.

Daily invest in your Spiritual growth. Praise and prayer are necessary for our relationship with God to develop. As we develop our relationship with God, our spirit is transformed from glory to glory (2 Cor 3: 18). Your spirit will be encouraged, built up, strengthened and the life of Christ will fill your being. You will be living in the Spirit. Reading scripture is not only necessary to sustain your spirit but the Word of God can be quickened as a RHEMA (living) Word to you so that you receive divine inspiration that can release blessings in your life. I mean things such as strength or encouragement but also things such as God will provide for all my needs. You will release in the spirit what must be released so that things such as a job, finances, transportation etc. will be released to you. First, they are released in the Spirit. It comes through the Word of God. You must know what God promises you before you can claim the blessings of the Word.

Scripture

Scripture is often referred to as "our daily bread". You must love God's word more than anything on earth to truly receive the blessings of it. Reading the Bible is not just something we do because we should. We read the Bible so that we might know God more. God is eternal. His word is established in heaven. He gives us His will expressed in the pages of the Bible. His care for us and the covenants He has made with people are in it. His covenant with us as believers in Jesus Christ makes us heirs of promise. The blessings of Abraham are given to us through Jesus Christ. The blessings of Israel through Jacob transformed by God into Israel are for us. Reading God's word and having it jump off the page at you because of the Holy Spirit living in you interpreting the Scripture to you is a joy not like any other. God desires to speak to us. God wants to teach us. The most usual way is through the scriptures.

If you are in a rough spot, search the scriptures for scriptures that give God's answers to your situation. Example, if you need finances, pray thanking God for supplying all your needs according to His riches in glory. You can use a concordance or an online app or tool such as Bible Gateway that has copies of many versions of the Bible as well as commentaries as well as a concordance etc.

Christian friends

Christians should have some Christian friends who can encourage you. They should be people who love God's Word and live radically to serve and honour God. If you do not have friends such as these, pray and ask God to place some in your life. They cannot do what you must do but they can encourage you as you build up yourself in God. Ungodly friends can hinder you. They will not be in agreement with you. I am talking about people who want to live in the light of God's presence and be living in victory with joy and living the best life possible.

Christian Ministries

Should you have a strong Christian friend share with him or her your situation. True godly people, will pray for you and with you. They will want God's best for your life. It is not a sign of weakness to ask for prayer. It is a sign of knowing you belong in the body of Christ. Other members of the Body of Christ will pray for you and it will release angels to protect you.

You may need to recruit some friends. Because I was the first Christian in my family, I often relied on Christian Broadcasting for my Christian family support. I learned the values of partnership with Christian ministries and have often sent prayer requests to them, knowing that they are people of integrity and they pray for their partners and they often hire people or people volunteer to pray over the requests. Please consider Christian ministries to get to help you to pray through a tough situation.

Faith

Sometimes you must build up your own faith by reading, confessing, praying and keeping in front of you, scripture. Get the scriptures on the inside of you. It isn't enough to memorize the scripture. You must see it fresh, say it fresh and pray it claiming it over your own life. You build up yourself by living in the Spirit.

Hebrews 6: 6 And without faith it is impossible to please God, for he who comes to God must believe that He exists and that He is a rewarder of those who diligently seek Him.

Get dressed for the occasion

It is important to wear the right clothes to the right occasion. For work, your clothes are usually different than your clothes for doing chores around the home. Soldiers wear different clothing in battle than they do on the army base for routines. The Bible commands us to dress appropriately for our Christian lives.

Ephesians 6: 11 Put on the whole armor of God that you may be able to stand against the schemes of the devil. 12 For our fight is not against flesh and blood, but against principalities, against powers, against the rulers of the darkness of this world, and against spiritual forces of evil in the heavenly places.

The Apostle Paul lets us know that as we live a Christian life, we are going to be fighting. The enemy is not people, although people may be used. The real enemy is the devil and demons. The truth is Jesus Christ triumphed gloriously over them. We have the victory through Jesus Christ.

I do not believe the Apostle Paul's word is merely an analogy. I believe just as soldiers dress for battle, we as Christians should dress appropriately. I literally pray on myself as though I were getting dressed- the armour of God. I literally believe there is spiritual armour that covers us spiritually to protect us. God told us to pray it because He knew there would be situations in our lives where we need it. What we see with our natural eyes may seem to be a natural thing, but if we were given a divine perspective of the situation, we would see things as they truly are in the spirit realm. There is a warfare of demons and angels of God. Rarely do we see it in our lives except through the Holy Spirit's discerning of spirits.

Ephesians 6: 13 Therefore take up the whole armor of God that you may be able to resist in the evil day, and having done all, to stand. 14 Stand therefore, having your waist girded with truth, having put on the breastplate of righteousness, 15 having your feet fitted with the readiness of the gospel of peace, 16 and above all, taking the shield of faith, with which you will be able to extinguish all the fiery arrows of the evil one. 17 Take the helmet of salvation and the sword of the Spirit, which is the word of God.

In the following passage, Elisha sees the spiritual realm but his servant can only see the invading physical army coming against them. He prays that his servant may see the angels. The angelic realm that was hidden to him becomes visible and the servant's faith is multiplied because of it. Divine perspective always brings clarity to human perspective. Knowing that God is with you and that His angels surround you always gives you boldness.

2 Kings 2: 15 When a servant of the man of God rose early in the morning and went out, a force surrounded the city both with horses and chariots. And his servant said to him, "Alas, my master! What will we do?"

16 And he said, "Do not be afraid, for there are more with us than with them."

17 Then Elisha prayed, "Lord, open his eyes and let him see." So the Lord opened the eyes of the young man, and he saw that the mountain was full of horses and chariots of fire surrounding Elisha.

It is not just a nice saying that God's angels will guard over you. It is a spiritual reality. There are guardian angels; there are angels who listen to

God's word from your mouth and bring it to come to pass. Angels will enforce God's Word when it is spoken in faith. There are ministering angels that intervene and make passage ways clear for you in the spiritual realm. In the realms of the earth there are angels and demons. It will be this way until Jesus Christ returns. Christians, however, have been given authority to bind and cast out demons. We release God's ministering spirits by faith in God who gave us angels to guard over us.

Psalm 91: 11 for He shall give His angels charge over you
    to guard you in all your ways.

Jesus defeated the devil and demons by his death, burial and resurrection. He ascended into Heaven and promised to return to earth. He commanded us to share the gospel all over the earth. He also gave us all authority to live an earth even as He is God.

Matthew 28: 18 Then Jesus came and spoke to them, saying, "All authority has been given to Me in heaven and on earth. 19 Go therefore and make disciples of all nations, baptizing them in the name of the Father and of the Son and of the Holy Spirit, 20 teaching them to observe all things I have commanded you. And remember, I am with you always, even to the end of the age." Amen.

1 John 4: 17 In this way God's love is perfected in us, so that we may have boldness on the Day of Judgment, because as He is, so are we in this world.

Jesus gave us His authority in His name. at the name of Jesus, demons tremble and are cast out. At the name of Jesus, every knee will bow. That includes things of the earth and people, but it also includes the spirit realm. Jesus says something so awesome here that even as He is, so are we in the world. Jesus is the LORD God King of Kings. It is this same authority that God has given to us to live on earth. Knowing God's Word and His promises for us, gives us boldness to proclaim God's Word causing the enemy to leave. It is the authority of The LORD Jesus Christ that backs up scripture. Your faith in Jesus – Jesus Christ alone and His Holy Word make you more than a conqueror through Christ.

Non- Christians

Non-Christian cannot comprehend or understand, just as Elisha's servant did not understand until it was revealed to him. Non- Christians do not have a chance of fighting; that is why it is so important we pray for them that they may be saved. God will give them opportunities to receive

Jesus.

The Helmet of Salvation

First, we must protect the head. Helmets have been worn for centuries. A wound to the head can result in a death. We do not trust in any other helmet except the blood of Jesus Christ shed for us. The helmet of salvation is the blood of Jesus applied to our lives and our faith in the blood of Jesus. Jesus blood shed for us is our boldness. Jesus paid the price for our souls so that we could live eternally with God. The helmet of salvation protects us as Jesus blood is our righteousness. Knowing you have peace with God, gives you boldness. It is often called Holy boldness. It is not from us originally but has been imparted to us from Jesus Christ who died and rose from the dead and who is returning as he promised.

The helmet of salvation is through Jesus Christ and Christ alone. We cannot boast in anything accept that Jesus blood paid the price for our souls. It is not our faith because faith is a gift of God given by grace (Ephesians 2: 8-9). The helmet protects the brain. The helmet can protect you from any sin or temptation by causing you to think upon God's Word and to keep it first in your life (Ephesians 4: 8).

The Breastplate of Righteousness

The breastplate guards your heart. If you were see a suit of armour, you would see the breastplate is usually made of metal or tough thick leather. It means any attack to your main organs cannot penetrate you. There are excellent in depth teachings on the armour of God. I recommend you get it from Kenneth Copeland or Joyce Meyer. They go into much more detail than what I am doing in this book. I am only mentioning the parts here. A spear or sword through the heart means death. Protecting the internal organs in the front of your body is essential to protecting your life.

Guard Your heart

Proverbs 4: 23 Keep your heart with all diligence,
    for out of it are the issues of life.

The application of this word is not simply to pray covering but to keep your heart pure. Keep your heart in God's Word and focused on God. Throughout the book of Deuteronomy as the people are entering the promised land, God speaks to Moses and Moses reminds the people to obey God's commandments. They must keep the word of God in their eyes, their ears, their lives. They must live with purpose to hold onto God's Word as authority for their lives. God's Word engrafted into our very souls (James 1: 21) can keep us on the right path. Engrafting means to take something and integrate it so it becomes a living part of something else.

I am a gardener. I have engrafted branches into other trees. It means the gardener slices the branch in a V shape and the branch he or she is engrafting also into a V shape at the branch's end. It means the gardener puts the two together so the V shapes fit together. There is solution a person can buy to engraft them to help them to grow together. The gardener wraps the branches with duct tape or other tape. The branches will grow together and become as one. God's word must become a part of our lives so much that it becomes a living part of us, so that we become an living epistle.

O how we must protect our heart with God's Word. It matters what we take in through our senses. We should guard what we see, what we hear, what we give our affections to. The breastplate of righteousness is Jesus righteousness. I identify in Jesus' death and resurrection for my soul. I can say with boldness I am the righteousness of God in Jesus Christ (2 Corinthians 5: 21). I do not live in my own righteousness but in the righteousness of Jesus Christ. Jesus Christ lives in me and His righteousness lives in me.

Jesus never sinned not even one sin while he lived as a man on earth. Jesus gave his holy life for me that I might have righteousness imparted to me. He gave His life for me, for you, for every person that would believe in Him. He died so that we might live a Holy life. He died so that we can have relationship with God. God hates sin. Without Jesus, we cannot approach God because God is Holy. Jesus became our righteousness as He gave His life for us so that we could be a Holy people.

Years ago, I received an excellent teaching by Kenneth Copeland that has quickened God's word in me. He explained how the armour of God is really Jesus clothing us with Himself. His righteousness is our righteousness. Each piece of the armour is really God's protection over us. If we sin, we must repent immediately. Don't start saying you are a sinner; instead repent quickly and go to God. Because Jesus cleanses us and washes us, we live in the righteousness of Christ. Start thanking God you have been cleansed by the blood of Jesus and are made Holy by the blood. The devil and demons can only see us clothed in Jesus Christ's armour as long as we remain in Jesus Christ and live Holy. Living holy means you repent quickly and keep God's word first. Receive by faith Jesus Christ's forgiveness.

Receive by faith Jesus Christ's righteousness. Confess it with your mouth.

Girding your loins with truth

The loins area starts at the waist and covers the genitalia or sexual parts. It is essential that you cover this area in a sword fight because it is a vulnerable area. A coat of armour protects this area. It often appeared as a thick belt. Truth is essential in protecting our sexual areas and vital organs. The truth must be that we are without sin. There should be no sexual sin that weakens the girdle of truth. Jesus Christ is our righteousness. Claiming this truth is also living the truth. As we confess our sins, God forgives us, but that is not sufficient to stop sinning. We must replace the desire to sin with God's Word. His word engrafted into us is a weapon. We live sexually pure because it is God's commandment.

Preventative

Keeping yourself from even the temptation to sin is important. It matters what we take into our being. Many people do not realize they contaminate themselves by listing to music that is sexual or not spiritually up lifting. What we listen to matters. It goes into the heart of a person. Once I got saved, within a day the Holy Spirit prompted me to do some house cleaning. I knew that I knew I had to get rid of some occult books that I had (hundreds of dollars' worth). I knew I had to burn them.

Also, there was music. I had many vinyl records that I knew were not pleasing to God. I burned some and threw others out. I knew by God's Spirit that they were not pleasing to God. The day before I got saved, I never knew or would have understood why I should get rid of them. With the Holy Spirit, living inside of me, I knew those things were unclean. They were not going to help me know God. The books you read matter. The magazines and reading materials matter. You cannot be seeing naked pictures of people or sexual pictures and not be affected by it. You must get rid of these things so that you are not feeding garbage to your spirit.

If you sin, repent quickly!

If you sin, repent quickly. Do not hesitate to go to Jesus. He is the God who gave His life for you. Don't simply believe it is normal. Christian life should not be sinning. Christian life should be holy.

1 John 1: 9 If we confess our sins, He is faithful and just to forgive us our sins and cleanse us from all unrighteousness.

If you have sexual relations with a person, but are not married, and you love the person, marry the person. Don't believe the lie that it is okay to live together or to have sex together outside of marriage. Repent separately and repent together and from that moment on, keep pure until you marry. Do not give yourself to situations where you are alone in any type of sexually intimate way until you marry. You could get a marriage certificate and later once you've saved money, have a party and invite your friends to celebrate.

Receive the cleansing of Jesus blood for you. You could get the communion elements, bread and wine or juice and pray refreshing your commitment to Christ and partaking of the communion. Offer yourself to God as a living sacrifice (Romans 12:1 -2). If you do not feel forgiven, confess with your mouth God's Word. God's Word is always true. Your faith must be in God's word not in your feelings. Your body is a temple of the Holy Spirit. God's Spirit is living in you. Do not put yourself in any type of compromised situation. Determine in your spirit to live Holy and righteous for God. If you love the person and are sexually attracted – marry. If it is lust and you really don't want to marry the person, repent and get help from a mature Christian who will keep you accountable for your vow to serve Christ sexually pure.

If it is a habitual sin, you should pray for God to help you understand if it is an iniquity or something you are feeding on that is garbage. Iniquities are sins that run in families. It starts with people being hard hearted towards God and not repenting and continuously sinning. Someone in your family – it should be you, must repent for the sin and for the iniquity. The same blood that forgives you can cut off iniquity from your family.

God can also show you if there is some type of garbage your putting into yourself. Example, maybe you watch TV show because it is funny but it has sexual sin in it or other things that give a negative message. I understand it sounds radical, but it is radical. If you want to live without sexual sin, you must keep yourself pure. There are excellent clean and funny shows that you can watch on Christian TV or satellite. The Glory Star is a Christian satellite with over 70 stations on it. It includes stations for children and teens. There are documentaries, news programs, preaching and teaching and movies etc.

Do not let sin reign in you. You cannot allow garbage to go in you and not expect an outcome. Should you put the word of God in you, you are sowing to the Spirit. You will reap of the Spirit.

Whatever you sow into you will manifest in your life.

Galatians 6: 7 Be not deceived. God is not mocked. For whatever a man sows, that will he also reap. 8 For the one who sows to his own flesh will from the flesh reap corruption, but the one who sows to the Spirit will from the Spirit reap eternal life.

No Other gods

Exodus 20: 3 You shall have no other gods before Me.

4 You shall not make for yourself any graven idol, or any likeness of anything that is in heaven above, or that is in the earth beneath, or that is in the water below the earth. 5 You shall not bow down to them or serve them; for I, the Lord your God, am a jealous God, visiting the iniquity of the fathers on the children to the third and fourth generation of them who hate Me, 6 and showing lovingkindness to thousands of them who love Me and keep My commandments.

You may not be worshipping other gods knowingly, but keeping any image of them or token from that other religion is sin against God. I myself did a pretty major house cleaning not only the day after I got saved but continuously afterwards as I had an interest in the supernatural and had collected various idols and symbols of other gods. About two or three years after I had cleaned and removed all that I believed I should get rid of, I was praying. I had been taught much of the word of God from excellent Bible classes and a healthy Church atmosphere.

I had my life transformed by God's Spirit. I was in prayer, not about the matter of idols at all, when suddenly God showed me a piece of jewelry I had that was to a false god. I saw it and I saw its exact location. I knew I had to get rid of it. I did. Things from other gods, or religions, give a point of access to demonic spirits. You must get rid of them. Should you earnestly pray, God help me; if there is any possession or thing that is unpleasing to you, show it to me and I will get rid of it. If you pray that way, God will certainly honour you and help you to spot things to get rid of.

Shoes of Peace

Isaiah 52: 7 7 How beautiful upon the mountains

are the feet of him who brings good news,

In the Bible, feet represent the walk of a person or the lifestyle of a person. A person bringing the good news of the gospel would be a person who shares Christ with others. It means you purpose to live for God and you walk it out in shoe leather. It means you live what you believe and are a living example of what you believe. In Elizabethan English "feet" is sometimes used to mean sex. It also means living with a pure, holy, walk.

Dig In

In the Roman army, the sandals they wore had a heavy claw like nail in the front so the soldier could dig in to the ground with it and be unmovable. Sure footing is essential in a fight. If the enemy can knock you down, it certainly gives an advantage. In our Christian lives, our walk must be holy. The things you do each day, the things you think about, the things you meditate on, the things that you give your efforts or affections to matter. Watching faith building videos feeds your spirit. Listening to encouraging Christian music or non-sexual, non- contaminated music matters. There is some secular music that is not negative and does not send a wrong message. Until you know the difference between it and the other – get Christian music. God will give you discerning of spirits once you are a Christian. Pray for it to become strong in your life so God can lead you.

You are a Temple

The places you go, you bring Christ with you. Most people believe this is awesome while they are at work or at school or at church. If you go to your old taverns and bars and non-Christian friends who are addicted to video games, or sex or drugs, or whatever, you are bringing Christ there. It is important that you severe any relationships that drag you into your sinful lifestyle. It is good to want to share the gospel with those people, but you cannot be doing what they are doing and expect to bring glory to God. You can invite these people to a different atmosphere, where you share what God has done in your life. I did this once I got saved. What happened is many people expected me to live the same way I did before. I had to make it clear to them that I was not the same because I had been born again. Those people wanted nothing to do with me and I wanted nothing to do with my old sinful self. It meant getting new friends.

True Friends

The people who became my friends took Bible classes with me. The people I served with at Church and teammates from Church sports teams etc. became my friends. I treasure those friends because we had Jesus Christ as the foundation of our relationship. These are people I could talk to, pray with and worship with as well as enjoy concerts, picnics, movies and other entertainment with. A whole new sphere of people were in my life. It didn't develop suddenly. It developed over the years as we shared life together as Christians. These are the types of people who will stay your friends throughout your life adding value to you and will encourage you to live for God.

Daily Walk

There are some Christian ministries that have this title on their websites. It means daily devotional life as a Christian. You do not pray or read scripture because you have to. You do not go to church because you have to. You do these things because Jesus Christ becomes your passion and you want to live pleasing to him. Once you receive a revelation of God's overwhelming grace towards you, you will become so thankful that words in English or your native language cannot express it. You will be overwhelmed with thanksgiving and it will cause you to seek God first. You will realize the only joyful abundant life is to be living in Jesus Christ.

You do not have to choose Jesus Christ. Yes, He is the way, the truth and the life, but you could choose a sinful way. You will never know freedom or true joy unless you choose the freedom that only Jesus Christ can give. Jesus Christ set me free. I can tell you; He radically transformed me. I'm like a different person. I started to want more of God the closer I got to Him. As I pressed in, He set me free of bondages of sin and of surface level living. The Holy Spirit becomes the Teacher and He shows you the right ways to go. The Holy Spirit will prompt you to go or warn you not to go. God lives on the inside of you and He will be your Senior Partner should you let Him.

Holy Spirit Led life

In Business, the Senior partner is the only who owns the business and makes the decisions. Junior partners are welcomed but it isn't frequently or without proving yourself etc. The Senior partner is the decision maker and the person who has the reputation to make the business a success. David Yonggi Cho, a pastor of the largest congregation in the world of at least 900, 000 people wrote a book called The Holy Spirit: My Senior Partner. I highly recommend it to you. It describes submitting to the Holy Spirit to teach you and lead you. Pray and ask the Holy Spirit to show you the right way and to prompt you to repent should you say anything or do anything that is not pleasing to God. The Holy Spirit will do it. He never forces us. Even if it were to save our human lives, God would never force us to do anything. He prompts us; He speaks to us but never forces. You ultimately make the decision. Should you pray, Holy Spirit be my Senior partner, He will do it.

Living in the Spirit

If you are a single Christian, you should be living for Christ with all your being: spirit, soul and body. You should be doing your best in your school or your job and keep fixed on Jesus Christ as your role model. Give. Serve. Encourage others. Your life should be living wholly set apart for God. As a single Christian, you can visit the elderly; you can help your parents with chores; you can witness to those who don't know Christ; you can give yourself to serving at church or in the community.

Give yourself wholly unto God: God will use you and teach you and give you a life so fulfilling words cannot explain it. You may meet your husband or wife in one of those situations. Don't focus on getting married. Focus on living for Christ with all of your being. I have done so myself and have known others who will give their priorities and their affections to God and serving, teaching, giving etc. Align yourself with the Word of God. Fix your life on living unto Christ and expect God to fill you, use you and give you the most joyful exciting life possible.

1 Thessalonians 5: 23 May the very God of peace sanctify you completely. And I pray to God that your whole spirit, soul, and body be preserved blameless unto the coming of our Lord Jesus Christ.

The Standard

Christians are held to a higher standard than the average person. We live with Christ living in use. God will clearly teach you what things are pleasing to Him and what things are not. The more of yourself that you give to God, the more He will live in you and you will be stronger, free, joyful, abundantly blessed. I mean God can give you favour that is so amazing that blessing keep coming your way. We are to live a holy life. We are to uphold the laws of our land such as paying taxes and doing the speed limit etc. But we are held to a higher standard as we are to do it with excellence shinning as lights of Christ's love in the earth.

Christians are to be the standard bearers for our society. Just as in the

Olympics opening ceremony the athletes carry flags of their nations, so we as Christians, carry the standard of the LORD Jesus Christ. We live giving; we live serving; we love others; we are living for God. True Christians are people of integrity; they keep their word. They live with boldness and humility and excellence. The standard is to live as a leader no matter what position you are in. You lead with a good attitude and righteous lifestyle.

Consistency

There should be consistency in prayer. It is a relationship. It is not a duty. The lie is that it is a duty. We pray because there is communion with God. We are the friends of God. God fills us and manifests His presence in us. It is our lifestyle, not something unimportant. Gloria Copeland said it and it was absorbed by my spirit. In consistency is the power. It is not the occasional prayer or occasional reading of God's word that makes a difference but the constant habitual practice of living for God that makes the difference.

Shield of Faith

The shield was so important in battle because it protected the soldier from the blows of a sword or spear. The shield is faith. Faith in the Word of God. It protects us and is also a tactical force if a person is in battle. Faith in the Word of God, faith in the blood of Jesus, faith in His covenant with you – gives you boldness against any enemy. Faith should be the strongest force in your life. Without faith you cannot please God.

Hebrews 11: 66 And without faith it is impossible to please God, for he who comes to God must believe that He exists and that He is a rewarder of those who diligently seek Him.

You may say that you want to have faith but you don't have it. The good news is you can get it. Faith comes by hearing the word of God. Hearing the Word of God preached is an excellent way of building up your faith.

Romans 10: 17 So then faith comes by hearing, and hearing by the word of God.

Build up your Faith

I would highly recommend getting faith scriptures and scriptures about the situation you are in and playing them over and over. Your hearing the Word, seeing it, and saying it with your mouth, as well as praying it, make all the difference to you. The Word of God has within it the potential to bring itself to come to pass. It is the inspired word of God. It is God's word filled with the life of God. The Holy Spirit in you grabs on to the word and quickens you in your spirit releasing faith.

There have been occasions where I had an excellent message preached, a RHEMA Word that was directly to me. I bought the tape or CD and played it over and over again. The Word of God kept encouraging me all throughout the week. Sometimes, I would listen to it more than a week. I had at least 1 hour travel and I played that CD over and over. What happens as you hear the Word is that new revelation comes to you and you can get faith for more areas of your life as you hear it and hear it over again.

Other times, I taped my own voice reading scriptures that were exactly about my situation and I listened to them over and over. I was feeding my own spirit on God's Word. It was especially made for me. I knew it was God's Word that was releasing faith inside of my spirit. It strengthened me. I have given CD's to people who needed physical healing or a health miracle and the CD's played constantly releasing life into their rooms.

Faith does not come from earth. It comes from Jesus Christ sitting on the throne of glory. It comes from The Holy Spirit who lives inside of you. Faith is a supernatural force. All things are possible to them who believe. That means no weapon fashioned against you can prosper. It means that you can do all things through Christ who strengthens you. It means God always causes you to triumph through Christ Jesus. Because faith is a spiritual force of God's life and resurrection power, you can use it as a shield to defend yourself against any attack from an enemy. Read over those scriptures and confess them until they automatically come up from your heart.

If you can't do much, do something

There were days all I could do is hold on to my Bible and say "I believe. I believe". I know what it like to lose a loved one. I know what it like to bury your closest relatives. God's Word is what I held onto. If that is all you can do, do it. Hold onto God's Word and pray for His mercy. Plead the blood of Jesus over yourself. Do something to build up your faith. God will meet you at your point of faith.

We are spiritual beings and faith is the substance that flows through us. It is God's system like money is the currency on earth, faith is the currency of spiritual things and for answers to prayer. As water flows from a tap or a hose, so does faith flow from God's Word to our spirit as we believe it. We are meant to be a conduit for the Spirit of God. You are not to collect faith like a cistern but you are to let it flow like a fountain. One encounter with God is not enough. You should be daily living in the presence of God. Faith is strengthened and renewed each day as you pray the Word and confess it. It should be strong. You can't wait until you need faith to build it. You should be building up your faith each day so that in the day you need it, you are already stronger on the inside spirit man. You have your shield of faith and you can use it.

It includes every area of your life. It includes your leisure activities; it includes your job, your school, your public life, your private life. You need the armour of God with you anywhere you are. It is what protects us. As an astronaut requires a space suit every place he or she goes in space, we require the armour of God on us. It defends us and protects us; God's Word in our mouth is a shield that defends us. The Word is true and can cover us completely as a Roman shield was huge almost the size of the soldier.

Of course, it is good to have a friend to pray with, a prayer group to pray with, a church to pray for you. There are instances in every person's life where he or she has got to face a situation with faith in God. The Word that you put within you, builds you up and strengthens you. The words coming from your mouth should be God's Word. God's Word will defeat any foe. Angels are released to bring the Word to come to pass. Your faith in the Word as you speak it takes authority over your soul and your body.

Daily Praise and Prayer and Worship

Reinforce the shield of faith with prayer and praise. Get up and praise and worship God with all your being each day. Praise Him in English. Praise Him in tongues. Thank Him for what He has done for you in the past. Thank Him for protecting you in the present. Thank Him for protecting you in the future. God strengthens you as you praise and worship – faith is released. God may speak a Word to you or it may come up out of your spirit – a scripture or psalm or song that will energize and revitalize you. Do it today. Do it the next day and the next day as long as you are on the earth, or if you are an astronaut, in the realms of the earth. God will release joy in you as your worship and your faith will be strengthened.

Shield of faith protects

Not only can you use the shield of faith in battle, but God surrounds you with a shield of His protection because you are a Christian. There are angels that oversee your safety.

Psalm 5: 12 For You, Lord, will bless the righteous;
   You surround him with favor like a shield.

Angels keep a Hedge of Protection

I have been in situations where I almost died, near misses and possibly occasions for death but God has delivered me. An example, I believe many people not only myself could bring would be I was going on my usual route but suddenly felt strongly that I should go a different way or I had a prompting to stop or I forgot something and had to retrace my steps. Later, I found out that if I had kept going my usual way, a truck had overturned or some incident happened and because of my prompting to go a different way, I avoided the danger completely. I don't believe it is a coincidence. I believe God sent angels to help me and steer me to safety.

One incident happened and I knew God's angels protected me. I was on a busy highway going about 60 mph and it was winter. I tried to stop and there was ice. My car did a spin around; I was on the highway (it was a one-way highway) completely turned in the opposite direction. As I spun around I prayed 'O Jesus help me' or something like it. To my amazement, I did not hit any other car. There were suddenly no cars around me and I was able to get to safety. I knew God had protected me in that situation.

Learning to use the Shield

There have been situations where the Word of God was preached and I learned something that I never knew before and started praying it over myself. An example is that God desires to financially prosper His people. God lists poverty as a curse and prosperity as a blessing. I remember when I first heard that. Thank God for Kenneth Copeland. I had some good teaching about God will supply your needs but I didn't know God would give me the desires of my heart. I didn't realize that by God prospering me, He receives all the glory. It is His desire to prosper me. Because of prosperity, I can give to the gospel more and I can give to people more.

2 Corinthians 9: 11 So you will be enriched in everything to all bountifulness, which makes us give thanks to God.

Shield of faith that God wants to prosper His people

As soon as I realized this new truth, that God wants to prosper me so I can be a giver and bless others, I started praying for God to prosper me and to give me the right heart attitude so I could receive and give and be a blessing to others. Deuteronomy 28 talks about the blessings and prosperity and earthly wealth promised to His covenant people. It talks about the blessings of obeying God and the possible curses. I started praying specifically over areas of my life for God to supply all my needs according to His riches in glory. Some religions believe poverty is being spiritual. It is the direct opposite of what's God word states. If I had a bill or a cost, I would start praying to God to supply the finances. Mostly God gave me jobs so that I could earn money. Almost always, whenever I had a need, I prayed and God gave me a job, or an extra job or the opportunity to earn the finances.

Miraculous Answer to Prayer

There were unusual opportunities also. One such is remarkable. I was caring for stray cats; there were about 35 - 39 of them. I was a student. I had a part time job but finances were tight. I would spend my extra money to buy cat food. One day I had used the last of the cat food. There was none left but I didn't have any money left either. I remember praying about it most seriously expressing it to God, believing that he had given me the heart to care for them. I prayed strong claiming His intervention. My shield that day was that God would supply my needs.

Within one hour I was standing on my front porch (a feeding area for the cats) and there were two women walking by. One of them stopped. They both stopped. The taller woman addressed me and asked me if I was the owner of all the cats. I hesitated to agree with it. She asked again in a slightly different way. I said Yes. She approached the porch and said " I believe God wants me to give this to you.". She handed me fifty dollars. I didn't know her. She didn't know me. God used her to supply. I thanked her and said God bless you to her. I only saw her on one other occasion while I was visiting a church. She didn't even recognize me. God used her. I bought enough food for the next month; it was many years ago and it would be comparable to perhaps 300 dollars today. I didn't have too many of those occasions. Usually, God gave me job opportunities.

Sword of the Spirit

Hebrews 4: 12 For the word of God is alive, and active, and sharper than any two-edged sword, piercing even to the division of soul and spirit, of joints and marrow, and able to judge the thoughts and intents of the heart.

The word of God is much more than words on paper. It is a historical document but it more; it is a worship document, but more; it has God's expressed will concerning our lives. God's Word is inspired by the Holy Spirit; it expresses the will of God; as we read it the Holy Spirit can teach it to us. As the Word is mixed with faith it becomes a powerful weapon. We speak that word with authority and it brings supernatural intervention.

People may fight against you but the real enemy is the devil. The people may not even know the devil is using them to fight you. As you answer with the sword of the word of God, you get to the root or source of the issue. God's word slays the real enemy and may amaze and perplex the people who are fighting you. The real enemy is the devil and demons. They were cast down out of heaven. They hate us because God loves us. The only way to fight in the spirit realm is to use God's weapons: His Word, His blood, His name, the Spiritual gifts.

2 Corinthians 4: 4 For the weapons of our warfare are not carnal, but mighty through God to the pulling down of strongholds, 5 casting down imaginations and every high thing that exalts itself against the knowledge of God, bringing every thought into captivity to the obedience of Christ,

If you are faced with a situation of some person fighting against you, for no reason, pray for God to quicken a word to you so that you may speak it. It will immediately disarm your enemy. I have seen certain special force agents who can disarm a villain within moments. The Word of God can do it as well. I have had several such occasions in my life where God quicken a scripture to me and suddenly the person who was fighting me verbally or abusing me verbally was completely stunned and unable to continue. Quickly they departed. God's Word can shut the mouth of your enemy. If they are saying bad things about you, use the Word of God. Don't try to fight it in the natural. Use God's Word. Fight the right way – the fight of faith by using God's Word. God backs his words. Angels are released to bring the word of God to come to pass. As you speak it in faith, angels bring it to pass. Nothing can stand against you as you speak God's Word with faith.

Isaiah 54: 17   No weapon that is formed against you shall prosper, and every tongue that shall rise against you in judgment, you shall condemn.

This is the heritage of the servants of the Lord,
  and their vindication is from Me,
  says the Lord.

Clothe yourself in God's armour as you pray each day. If necessary remind yourself of it throughout the day. Keep in an attitude of prayer knowing that God can speak to you and help you throughout your day. Being dressed in God's armour is a must for every believer to live a victorious life. It is the first way to encourage and build yourself up. It is being fully dressed for the occasion. Each day of life is a new opportunity from God.

2 ENCOURAGING YOURSELF IN GOD

Jude 1: 20 But you, beloved, build yourselves up in your most holy faith. Pray in the Holy Spirit. 21 Keep yourselves in the love of God while you are waiting for the mercy of our Lord Jesus Christ, which leads to eternal life.

I live in Canada. There are four seasons: winter, spring, summer and fall. Some people hate the changes in weather. I myself like them. The changing of seasons causes us to prepare in special ways: for instance, the clothing we ware is different in the summer than in the winter or fall or spring. It also means changes around the home and different tools and equipment we need in winter rather than in summer.

There are seasons in God where there are messages preached from the pulpit that inspire and release faith in you. Your friends or family may be around to encourage you with scriptures or prayer. There are opportunities in each person's life where he or she must stir up the gift of faith. You must know how to build up yourself in the most Holy faith. It may mean that you need extra Word so you supplement your church services with Christian Media. It might mean fasting and praying. It might mean, getting up earlier to worship more or praise more. The Holy Spirit will prompt you to do something different. It may mean that you invest in books and materials to spark your faith. The largest part of it is that you recognize the need and the prompting of the Holy Spirit.

You know you are in the right church if the pastors who are preaching are directly imparting encouragement, exhortation, comfort and inspiration to you as he or she preaches. In my early Christian years, in my 20's, I attended a church where the word spoken from the pulpit seemed to target my heart completely each week. It was a supernatural provision from God of spiritual nutrients that strengthened me, taught me, encouraged me etc. Just as God supplied manna in the wilderness that fed the people of Israel, for forty years, God provides for us spiritual manna in the word of God. Usually, it comes from your pastor.

Exodus 16: 4 Then the Lord said to Moses, "Indeed, I will rain bread from heaven for you. And the people shall go out and gather a certain amount every day, that I may test them, whether they will walk in My law or not. 5 And it shall come to pass that on the sixth day they shall prepare that which they bring in, and it will be twice as much as they gather daily."

THE RHEMA WORD

In my early 20's as a new Christian, I did not know there was any other way to live. I believed I could pray and read my Bible and get fed at Church each week. That was my early Christian life. I believed all people received all they needed from their Christian Church. I have learned since that it is possible to go to a Church where you receive only moments of inspiration not a RHEMA word from God. A RHEMA Word from God is the pastor prays and hears God specifically give him or her instruction to speak to the congregation. It is as manna that can feed children, youth, adults, new Christians, mature Christians etc.

RHEMA WORD

I did not know that I myself could pray and worship God at home and hear God's voice instructing me in specific precise ways satisfying me and strengthening me. It is not the pastor alone that makes the difference; it is the Word of God and prayer and praying for God to reveal the Word to you personally that makes the difference. Often when a person gets a word from God directly, it releases joy, faith, and energy – all aspects of knowing God and communing with Him in relationship. It is necessary to adopt the habit of prayer and praise each day. Reading the Word of God not just out of duty but because you want to know God's Word and receive of the treasures of it. There is joy released that is increasing and builds up your faith. Often, I have read the Word of God out loud and as I read it claimed it for myself.

For example, if I was reading Psalm 91 and it was quickened to my spirit by the Holy Spirit, it would release faith and the Word of God mixed with faith always produces life. I would read the Word out loud, thank God for the Word and confess it over myself.

Psalm 91: 11 for He shall give His angels charge over you
    to guard you in all your ways.

An example would be saying " Thank you that you assign guardian angels over me to protect me." A RHEMA Word is God revealing the Word to the human spirit as a revelation. The believer grabs onto the Word and claims it for his or her own life by faith. The faith mixed with the Word of God releases joy, peace, encouragement, strength etc.

You Can get your own RHEMA

I had been a Christian for several years when I was at home alone, the only Christian in my family, mid-week, with no way to get to my church (1 hour away) and I longed to hear God's Word. I believed I had to get to the church for it to occur. I wanted to praise and worship God and receive of the blessings of getting spiritually fed. The Holy Spirit spoke to me clearly that I could praise God at home.

The Holy Spirit taught me that I could praise and worship God wherever I go because God is in me. I remember the day. I started thanking God for the new revelation. I began to sing praise songs from church. I thanked God and praised God and praised God in tongues. I felt the overwhelming peace of God's presence. I got my Bible and prayed for God to speak to me. As I read the scripture, with faith and expectancy, God quickened the Word of God to me and I received spiritual encouragement. The Holy Spirit was with me teaching me, directing me and comforting me.

O please don't try to cheapen the relationship you have with God. You cannot simply open the Bible and point your finger and say – O I claim it. You cannot simply get a passage from the popular resource the daily bread and it be enough for you. You have got to pursue God as you would your closest friend. It is intimacy with God that gives us revelation and encouragement. If you are too busy to pray or read God's Word, you are too busy. I have learned that God is my strength. His presence with me, His encouragement to me through both relationship and the Word of God are precious to me. God is my strength.

Prayer

That doesn't mean that there may be seasons where I don't need more. For instance, a yearning for more of God means you should make sacrifices of your leisure life so you are pursue God more. Any time I have had these feelings of a calling towards God, I have obeyed knowing that I would be strengthened and built up. It might mean more prayer in tongues. Praying in tongues is the best possible way for yourself should you be sensing a feeling of yearning for God.

Romans 8: 26 Likewise, the Spirit helps us in our weaknesses, for we do not know what to pray for as we ought, but the Spirit Himself intercedes for us with groanings too deep for words. 27 He who searches the hearts knows what the mind of the Spirit is, because He intercedes for the saints according to the will of God.

Isaiah 55: 11 so shall My word be that goes forth from My mouth;
   it shall not return to Me void,
but it shall accomplish that which I please,
   and it shall prosper in the thing for which I sent it.

I want my faith to become instant. The Word of God mixed with faith coming from a believer is praying the answer to the situation. It may bring forth 30, 60 or 100-fold.

Matthew 13: 8 But other seeds fell into good ground and produced grain: a hundred, sixty, or thirty times as much.

Matthew 13: 23 But he who received seed on the good ground is he who hears the word and understands it, who indeed bears fruit. Some produce a hundred, sixty, or thirty times what was sown."

Go for the 100-fold

The seed is essential. It is the Word of God. It has within it the power to make itself come to pass. The seed is always excellent. God's Word is always excellent. The condition of the soil makes a difference on the ability of the seed to grow. If the ground is cement. The seed may sprout but not be able to take root. If the soil is rocky, the seeds get caught up with the rocks and cannot grow fully. If the soil is rich and prepared so all rocks and weeds are removed, the seed can grow to full potential. Full potential is 100-fold. That means I plant one seed of corn and get a stalk of corn with hundreds of seeds in it (Matthew 18: 13-23).

The Word of God can bring 100-fold results in any area of your life that you mix it with faith. It concerns your salvation, your healing, your deliverance, your possessions, your finances, and in all spheres of authority of your life. O I want the Word of God to be producing 100-fold in me. I thank God for all growth but I will give myself wholly unto God with my heart pure before Him so that I can receive the 100-fold blessing on the Word of God I receive.

When I first heard these words, I thought it only applied to teaching in general. I thought it was a vague promise from God to hold onto God's Word. That was mostly because that is what I heard preached. I should keep my heart pure so I could receive the teaching and preaching from the pastor. As God revealed to me that I could apply the scripture to every area of my life, my excitement and expectation grew and my faith jumped to a new level. I knew that God could and would bless me in all areas of my life, not only in general ways but in very specific ways such as finances, or healing of a loved one, or words of wisdom or opportunities. God cares about every are of our lives and His Word is the provision He gives us for any need.

Christian Alliances

Align yourself with Christian Broadcasting that feeds you spiritually. Trinity Broadcasting Network, Day Star Christian Network, GOD TV CBN Broadcasting etc. – all of these are major Christian broadcasters who have got hundreds of faith filled preachers and teachers of the gospel on them. Also, there are Christian movies and documentaries and all sorts of Christian alternatives to regular TV.

I am saying regular TV rarely has true family based entertainment; it is doubtful you will be encouraged watching non-Christian programming. Align yourself with some Christian networks that can feed you spiritually, encourage you and connect you to others who believe the same. Some of them are Free To Air stations; some are satellite; some are on cable or regular TV. On the Internet, you can watch any of these stations. You can encourage yourself with Christian allies. God can get you the necessary Word you need through the right people.

Christian Media

I have mentioned Christian Media in each book I have written because I truly thank God for Christian media and the Body of Christ who preach and teach Christ on satellite or radio or television or cable etc. I received the most encouragement throughout the week through Christian media. I was the first Christian in my family. Christian media presented me with people of like precious faith including apostles, prophets, evangelists, pastors and teachers.

For several years I enjoyed the Glory Star a Christian satellite with over 70 stations including children's, teens', adults, ministry as well as Christian movies and documentaries, Christian news, Christian preaching. There are ministers who I have watched for decades that have spoken truths that have impacted my spiritual growth. God revealed to me I should give financially to them because they were directly feeding my spirit. Those preachers became my Christian family.

Christian Media made a difference in my life more than mere words can ever express. Imagine how much more the value could the Christian Media be to shuts ins who cannot get to church at all. Truly I thank God for the freedom to share Christ openly in North America. No Christian ever has to be alone. If you have a prayer request, there are ministers who will pray with you on the phone or you could send in your prayer requests through mail or from their websites. The sense of community and belonging and feeling a part of the Body of Christ came to me because of Christian media. Please realize, I developed Christian friendships. I became involved in my local churches. I was not cut off from the Body of Christ. Christian media has been an essential part of my Christian life.

Give to those who Feed you Spiritually

Please receive a nudge in your spirit, that if you have been blessed by a Christian ministry or minister. The TV program was a spiritual encouragement to you, to support that ministry in at least two ways. Pray for the ministry. If you received spiritual life from the ministry, give financially. I'm not going to tell you what to give. Pray and ask the Holy Spirit what you should give.

1 Corinthians 9: 11 If we have sown for you spiritual things, is it a great thing if we shall reap your material things?

There have been TV preachers that God has used to speak a RHEMA Word of God to me. It was just as if the Word was exactly what I needed because it was. God used the Apostle or Prophet, Evangelist, Pastor or Teacher as he would if I were there in person. God gave me the exact message that would jump start my faith. I knew God was speaking to me. I knew that minister was being used by God. If there are ministries that God uses to directly encourage you, you should consider becoming a partner. A partner is someone who regularly gives to the ministry.

Don't let anyone but the Holy Spirit prompt you of how often to give or how much to give. You may determine it yourself. If there is a ministry that is a source of blessing to your life, and you totally align with the beliefs of the ministry, pray for the Holy Spirit to reveal to you how much you should give. Please realize it might be more than you ever thought of, especially if you have a motivation of giving.

When God first started prompting me to give to ministries it was sometimes all the spare money I had. Sometimes, an amount larger than what I had would come to me. I knew it was correct, but it was beyond what I had. I would pray, God, if you give me the finances, I will give it. It didn't come instantly, but it did come. It came through faith and often when I pray about finances, God gives me a job or an extra job. That is the most usual way God supplies my finances for living as well as giving.

Tithing

Malachi 3: 10 Bring all the tithes into the storehouse, that there may be food in My house, and test Me now in this, says the Lord of Hosts, if I will not open for you the windows of heaven and pour out for you a blessing, that there will not be room enough to receive it. 11 I will rebuke the devourer for your sakes, so that it will not destroy the fruit of your ground, and the vines in your field will not fail to bear fruit, says the Lord of Hosts. 12 Then all the nations will call you blessed, for you will be a delightful land, says the Lord of Hosts.

Tithing is a way of spiritual protection. Give the tithe to the place you are being fed. Usually it is your local Church. Sometimes it is a ministry. God promises to supply your needs and to pour out blessings on your life more than you can hold. It means the first 10th of your income, you give to God through your local church or to a ministry that is feeding you. You do it with joy because God has prospered you and you obey his Word. Giving 10% is a command. As you do it, God fights against those who fight against you. God protects you in a special way; He rebukes the devourer. This ought to bring joy to you knowing God's covenant is with you because of Jesus Christ.

Giving above the tithe

There is joy in giving above the tithe. As God prospers you, and nudges your heart towards ministers who preach the gospel, you will want to give more than the tithe. You will understand that truly you can never out give God. Give your 10% but also give more. Pray that God will make you generous and prosper you so you can give more. God wants to entrust the finances of earth to those who believe in Him and those who will further the advancement of the gospel.

Luke 6: 38 Give, and it will be given to you: Good measure, pressed down, shaken together, and running over will men give unto you. For with the measure you use, it will be measured unto you."

You give in faith believing God to bless that ministry and to bless you and you will reap blessings beyond what words can express. If this topic offends you, please repent. Giving to the gospel so others can be spiritually fed and so that you can continue to be encouraged and so that the gospel will be carried north, south, east and west – is the will of God. Christians are the people who are going to finance the preaching of the gospel.

Blessed to be a blessing

Deuteronomy 8: 18 But you must remember the Lord your God, for it is He who gives you the ability to get wealth, so that He may establish His covenant which He swore to your fathers, as it is today.

Non-Christians are not going to want to give to the gospel. As a member of the body of Christ, you and I should be givers. Giving to promote the gospel can be through your local church missions, or through ministries that have blessed you or that you know are effectively preaching the gospel. It matters whom you give to. You should be in agreement with the ministry you give to. You should feel that the ministry is doing God's will by preaching and teaching. The ministry should align with the Word of God in all ways. As you give, pray for the ministry and pray that God will bless your giving of finances as a seed sown into the gospel. If you sow to the Spirit, you shall reap of the Spirit.

If you just begrudgingly give, don't expect to receive a blessing. Don't be vague about your prayers for that ministry. If possible pray a scripture over it. Don't just be vague about your seed. Thank God for supplying all your needs but say with boldness I give….. name the seed you are sowing. Believe God honours your faith because He does. Gove into the area you feel the need for. If you need healing, sow into a healing ministry. If you need finances, sow into a ministry that not only is a good steward but also preaches on sowing and reaping. Sow into your area of need, claiming your promise.

2 Corinthians 9: 7 Let every man give according to the purposes in his heart, not grudgingly or out of necessity, for God loves a cheerful giver.

The Holy Spirit

The only person who is with you every moment you need encouragement is the Holy Spirit. Keeping a close relationship with Him is most important. It will help you to stir up your own faith. Whether you are married, or single, the closest relationship in your life should be with God. God will always help you with all your other relationships. I wouldn't want to rely on my own supply of love or mercy or forgiveness. I thank God, I don't have to. I tap into the Holy Spirit who lives in me, God living in me, so that I can release the agape love of God, the mercy of God, the forgiveness of God towards people. God is my source.

Never believe the lie you are alone. You are a member of the body of Christ. If you joined to members of your local church but also to the whole Body of Christ on earth and in heaven. There are millions of people who believe in Jesus Christ. You are part of the Church of the living God. It matters that you speak to yourself that you know you are a member that belongs. It is important to have someone to agree with you in prayer though. Give your prayer requests to your closest Christian family and friends. Give them to your local Church. Give them to ministries that believe the same as you. Pray that God would bring people into your life who would agree with you in prayer about anything.

2 Peter 1: 1b To those who have received a faith as precious as ours through the righteousness of our God and Savior Jesus Christ.

People of like precious faith believe as you do and can agree with you 100% about your prayer request (as long as you are aligning with the scriptures.)

Psalm 119: 63 I am a companion of all who fear You,
and of those who keep Your precepts.

Pray for Christian companions. God can give you people who will agree with you in prayer for yourself or others. God can bring the right people into your life. You may go through periods where your closest support is from Christian Media. It is a provision for you. Receive it with joy. I had a friend who I met with for prayer regularly. We enjoyed such an awesome Christian friendship. Often, she was alone; her children had married and moved away and she was a widower. She had to make changes in her life to keep her spiritually fed. Something had to replace her efforts to care for her husband and children.

Prayer became a prime priority of her life. She joined several prayer meetings as well as scheduled some with me. She sang in the choir at her church. She volunteered in her church. She visited other churches. She was serving in her community. She was also somebody who received much from Christian media. There were several ministries she supported. One particular ministry was so special to her and encouraged her so much that she arranged for her vacations to be during those ministry conferences wherever they were held. She travelled all over the United States because of those ministry conferences. It brought such joy to her to gather with the ministry team and all the other partners (thousands) that would attend those meetings. She made friends from all over the USA. She is an example of somebody like myself who thank God for Christian Media.

If you are alone much, do not believe it will always be that way. I have known of so many widowers and widows who died within a year of their spouse because their lives were completely joined and the people felt no reason to live after the death of their spouse. Please do not be insulted by my comments but the truth is you are living; God is not done with your life. God will use you if you let Him. Grief is a horrible thing. I know what it is like to bury loved ones. I know what it is like to bury parents and family members. The scripture teaches us that as Christians we have hope non-Christians don't know about. We have God's promise that we will be united with our Christian family in the presence of Jesus Christ our Saviour.

1 Thessalonians 4: 13 But I would not have you ignorant, brothers, concerning those who are asleep, that you may not grieve as others who have no hope.

Fight Grief with God's Word

Don't let grief have any root in you. You do not have to live with it. It is more than mere positive thinking and it is most certainly not something any person can do in his or her own strength. Jesus our Messiah took upon Himself all of our sins. You know that. As a Christian, you by faith received it. Also, He died so that we might be healed. He can give beauty for ashes, the oil of joy for morning. These are not just words. These are God's promises and they are what Jesus Christ took upon Himself as he died on the cross, so that we could receive the blessings of peace, joy, health, comfort, etc.

Isaiah 61: 2 to proclaim the acceptable year of the Lord
    and the day of vengeance of our God;
to comfort all who mourn,
3   to preserve those who mourn in Zion,
to give to them beauty
    for ashes,
the oil of joy
    for mourning,
the garment of praise
    for the spirit of heaviness,
that they might be called trees of righteousness,

the planting of the Lord,
that He might be glorified.

Isaiah 53: 4 Surely he has borne our grief
and carried our sorrows;
Yet we esteemed him stricken,
smitten of God, and afflicted.
5 But he was wounded for our transgressions,
he was bruised for our iniquities;
the chastisement of our peace was upon him,
and by his stripes we are healed.

Jesus took upon himself our grief and sorrows. You may say, that is true but you don't know what I am feeling. The truth is God's Word is true. You must believe it by faith for it to manifest in your life. Read it over. Pray it and receive it by faith.

Fight Grief Like you Would fight Cancer

I have seen people possessed by it as a cancer that ultimately lead to a premature death. I have also known Christians who by faith received Jesus as LORD of all areas of their soul so that the application of the word of God comforted them and strengthened and healed them. Just as with any type of promise of God, you must have faith for it. You must pray it, confess it and take it in the spirit before it fully manifests in your life.

Hebrews 11: 6 And without faith it is impossible to please God, for he who comes to God must believe that He exists and that He is a rewarder of those who diligently seek Him.

I do believe Christian family and friends can help by prayer and kind words and doing activities with those who have lost loved ones or who need encouragement. It is essential that you believe God is bigger than anything- think about the omnipotence of God. It is tough on people who have been happily married for many years to lose a spouse. It is not impossible to continue to live and make a difference with your life though.

I would highly recommend Kenneth Copeland's book on grief and how to fight it in the Holy Spirit. Also, Joyce Meyers has some excellent teachings and books on deep inner healing from abuse. Her book "Beauty from Ashes" and her book " I was always on my mind" are both excellent testimonies of how God transformed her life from victim to victory. Not only was she healed by God but she preaches and teaches others the things she has learned. There are others who have been situations such as yourself. You should invest in yourself completely spiritually. You are worth it.

I wouldn't want to die prematurely and miss out on something I could have done for God. If you could live and make a difference by winning souls, serving people, encouraging people, giving etc. you should. God wants to use you. The reason you're on earth is the same but you must nurture and feed yourself the Word of God to build up your inner man. You've got to get teaching and preaching but you also have to get serious with God.

You've got to pray and fast and find out why you are living. I knew a widower in her 90's who gave herself to prayer and fasting. She didn't drive any more. Someone drove for her but she attended every prayer meeting she could get into. She was asked to preach quite regularly and she did. She poured herself into people who would get close to her knowing that God's anointing was on her mightily.

My single adult class were attracted to her like magnets to a target. As we talked about God, as we prayed together and as we learned from her, we encouraged her by our desire for the things of God. I'm emphasizing that there is no loss on earth that is worth dying for. Please receive this as a word of encouragement and exhortation. It is not a rebuke. I know by experience the human suffering of grief, but it doesn't have to dig its ugly roots into your life. You can fight it as you have fought any other thing – by faith.

Encouragers

If you know of a widower or widow, and you sow into his or her life God will bless you. If you will give encouragement. Literally search the scriptures and get an encouraging word and pray for the person, if possible go and visit the person and pray with him or her, God will release life in your spirit and life. Also, you will be enriched by your friendship with the person.

Galatians 6: 7 Be not deceived. God is not mocked. For whatever a man sows, that will he also reap. 8 For the one who sows to his own flesh will from the flesh reap corruption, but the one who sows to the Spirit will from the Spirit reap eternal life. 9 And let us not grow weary in doing good, for in due season we shall reap, if we do not give up. 10 Therefore, as we have opportunity, let us do good to all people, especially to those who are of the household of faith.

Sow into others

As you sow encouragement into others, as you volunteer and serve others in any way, God will always bless you more than you can give. The same principle that applies to money applies to all types of giving. Most certainly you can pray. Giving of your talents and your conversation will not only help those you give to but also build you up. What you sow you reap. Give to the area that you feel strongly about. For instance. If you have grandchildren, see if they need volunteers at their school. Should you feel a calling to prayer, commit yourself to prayer at home and with others. If you are able, volunteer to bake or to serve in your church or at a missionary organization or food bank.

Something most people never think of is the International Students that attend a University or College near you. Often, they are alone, away from home and you could invite one or two and give them a Thanksgiving dinner or even a special non-holiday meal. It would be good for them and also give you an interesting aspect of life. You will learn from them. You can make a friend from a different part of the world.

Schedule Yourself

It doesn't matter if you are young or not, you've got to plan a schedule so that you can start fresh after the loss of a loved one. Get yourself an Agenda book or a calendar. Plan yourself a schedule for your day and evenings. It includes prayer meetings, serving, church, family and friends. Now add to it Investment in self spiritually – that includes CDS or DVDS or books. Spend at least one hour a day in learning. I got that idea from John Maxwell. Many of his leadership teachings include personal development or lifelong learning. You should learn something new each day. You could take a course at school in something you've always wanted to study. You could go to the University or College library or the public library. Usually the University and college libraries have more variety of research materials.

Volunteer

I knew a widower who volunteered for many hours a week for many years. She did not brag about it. She simply volunteered at different churches and Christian organizations, the food bank, several cultural and ethnic organizations. She was given an award for her hundreds of hours of volunteer work. It was posted in the paper. That's how I found out. I knew she was active but I had no idea of all the fascinating helpful things she was doing until I saw it in the paper. I knew her because of Bible classes we took together. Some of her volunteer work was Christian but some was in her community. She purposed in her heart to live rather than die after her spouse died.

Self-Pity

Avoid self-pity as you would a plague. If it comes to you have scripture ready to fight it. Say the scripture out loud. Fight it with the best weapon available: God's Word.

Romans 8: 37 No, in all these things we are more than conquerors through Him who loved us.

There are many ministries that have scriptures organized by topic so you can pray specifically for the areas of need such as finances, overcoming fear, fighting grief etc. I can highly recommend the ones I have by Joyce Meyer, Marilyn Hickey, Benny Hinn and Jesse Duplantis. There are many more. I have only named some excellent ones that I use personally.

Fight self-pity because it leads to a spiral of death, hell and the grave all consequences of life on earth because of the curse upon Adam for sinning. Because of Adam and Eve sin came onto the earth and all humans were cursed with death and separation from communion with God. Jesus Christ delivered us from the curse of the law. Jesus Christ set us free. His victory is our victory. Use your mouth to align with God's Word. Don't speak negatively about yourself or about the situation or about any one. Line your words up with God's words.

Words

Proverbs 18: 21 Death and life are in the power of the tongue,
    and those who love it will eat its fruit.

It matters what we say about ourselves and about others. Words are containers for power. It can be awesome and it can be deadly. I knew a pastor who fascinated me by his saying he could talk to people for five minutes and find out their priorities in life.

An excellent way to handle the words of your mouth is to speak in line with God's Word. Kenneth and Gloria Copeland have excellent teaching on Confessions and the mouth. Joyce Meyer has excellent teaching on this topic including a couple of books. Joel Osteen has some excellent teaching on the topic of words and their impact.

If most people eliminated worthless talk, foolish talk, criticism and complaint, many people would talk less. That would not necessarily make them more joyful. Those things are indicators of a heart condition that is sinful and bitter. The answer is not simply talking less. It requires a whole transformation, a renewing of your mind. God's word must be engrafted into your heart so that the right words become a part of your life. It is not simply saying words. It comes from a total engrafting of God's Word into your heart. You become a spiritual man rather than a carnal Christian.

Romans 12: 1 I urge you therefore, brothers, by the mercies of God, that you present your bodies as a living sacrifice, holy, and acceptable to God, which is your reasonable service of worship. 2 Do not be conformed to this world, but be transformed by the renewing of your mind, that you may prove what is the good and acceptable and perfect will of God.

Gloria Copeland talks frankly about how God transformed her speech. She prayed "Holy Spirit line up my words with the Word of God. If I say anything displeasing, correct me. I am holding you accountable." God was faithful to His Word. The Holy Spirit would stop her or correct her words; she obeyed the Spirit and as a result her life was transformed. Her words were aligned with God's Word and her speech was encouraging, with faith, with purpose and to build up others.

The Holy Spirit will teach us and correct us if we ask Him. Jesus gave us the Holy Spirit to teach us, to lead us into all truth. He comforts us. He imparts the will of God to us. Your relationship with the Holy Spirit is necessary.

John 16: 13 But when the Spirit of truth comes, He will guide you into all truth. For He will not speak on His own authority. But He will speak whatever He hears, and He will tell you things that are to come.

Keep a Right Attitude

If you are playing sports and you lose, don't insult yourself or the team. Rather than focus on all the mistakes or errors, focus on what you could do. Have an attitude of I will improve. I will practice. I will give my best next game. We can do it. Your attitude matters. The words that come out of your mouth matter not only to your spirit but to those who hear you. Keep the attitude that nothing is impossible. You can do all things. Knowing that the resurrection power of Jesus Christ is in you should inspire you to greatness. You should know that God can help you do anything. Remember the ways He has lead you and protected you and delivered you in the past.

It doesn't mean you don't reflect on why you didn't win the game. You should. If possible remember it with your coach and your team. What should have been done. The coach's attitude can certainly make a difference in all of the team's attitude. If it was a different type of mistake or error, talk to the people involved. Remain positive. Give it your best. Talk to God about it to know how you can improve. Also, seek Him to see if there is some other way for you to make a difference. Maybe it means you give or serve or encourage. Maybe it means you try a different way. God can give you divine perspective of any situation so you can be viewing it from His point of view. Only God can truly show you the solutions.

Philippians 4: 13 I can do all things because of Christ who strengthens me.

I like winning. I hate losing, but I have learned that God will often give me new opportunities to improve and to win. I desire to develop and improve in all areas of my life that are important to me. These include things I do every day in my career and in my leisure activities as well as personal life. I am aiming for excellent. Should you aim for excellence, keep a positive attitude and continue to reflect and learn, you will continue to develop and improve. You will impact those around you within your sphere of influence.

Excuses

Don't take a loss blaming yourself or your team or other people by giving excuses. I mean don't avoid responsibility for the situation by saying "It's because of my parents." Or "It's because I was the only child". Your past, no matter how terrible it was does not have to influence your present or your future. Please I know some people have good reasons for being bitter or angry or resentful. If you were abused as a child or neglected or deprived or a parent died... all of these are excellent reasons to pity yourself. But self-pity is not of God.

It doesn't mean God doesn't care about you. He does. God can and will heal you of scars upon your soul. Please know God never planned those negative things to happen to you. Any negative things in your life are a result of people sinning. It goes back to Adam and Eve and original sin. Jesus blood not only saves you. Jesus is the healer. He can heal you of anything you have lived through.

2 Corinthians 5: 17 Therefore, if any man is in Christ, he is a new creature. Old things have passed away. Look, all things have become new.

Joyce Meyer

Joyce Meyer is an excellent example of a person whom God has healed. If anyone had excuses to be bitter and angry and gruff, she did. If you have not heard of her testimony of abuse and how God has transformed her from being self-absorbed and negative, please I encourage you to watch the DVDS of her testimony.

She had every excuse to be negative all of her life. If she did not let God heal her, she could have stayed negative, bitter and seething with anger. It would have been a hellish life for her. She obeyed the promptings of the Holy Spirit and learned about giving to others and caring for others. She started getting joy from giving and showing Christ's love by letting Jesus Christ live in her and through her. She was completely transformed and God blessed her ministry so that she can witness and preach the same Jesus that healed her that can heal any person. It is tough what I am saying. I am saying don't let anger or bitterness or self-pity have any place in your life. These things do not come from the Spirit of God. God's presence brings righteousness, peace and joy.

Romans 14: 17 For the kingdom of God does not mean eating and drinking, but righteousness and peace and joy in the Holy Spirit.

God can give you overcoming joy so that instead of your life being ruined by the devil, God can receive glory and honour because you have been healed and you use your healing to give testimony of the magnificence of Jesus Christ. You can be set free from your past. You can enjoy your life in the present and in the future. Don't believe the lie that you don't get a good life although others do. That's a lie. God saved you; He wants you to be set free so you can enjoy your life and thank God for every day of it. If you have had enough of self-pity, and feel conviction, pray a simple prayer of dedicating yourself to God.

John 8: 36 Therefore if the Son sets you free, you shall be free indeed.

[Prayer] Jesus

Thank you for saving me and providing for me. You know the things of my past. God have mercy on me and bring healing. Lead me to the right teachings and preaching and people who can speak words of truth to me that set me free from all negative self-absorption. Show me the riches of the knowledge of the glory of Christ. Reveal yourself to me. Amen.

Your true Inheritance

God can reveal to you your true inheritance in Jesus Christ. You are an heir of promise because of Jesus Christ. You are of the lineage of Abraham by faith. You are a member of the Body of Christ with a new lineage. Jesus redeemed us from the curse. You were born again into the family of God.

Galatians 3: 29 If you are Christ's, then you are Abraham's seed, and heirs according to the promise.

Jesus Christ can heal you so that there is no negative thorn in you. You can remember the past but there is no bitterness or hatred. You focus on your present and on how God's mercy has reached you. There is a certain type of race in the Olympics that includes hurdles. There are obstacles placed around the track and you have to jump over them as you run. It wasn't my best event but I could do it. It required much effort. There were others in my class who could leap over them like fawns without losing speed.

You don't have to let any hurdle of life stop you from the blessings of Abraham or the blessings God promised to His children through Moses. Jesus Christ took upon Himself all sin and inequity. He paid the price so you could be free from the curses of life. It means absolute trust in God. It means wholly giving all parts of yourself to God. God can give you laughter, joy, abundance and blessing. It comes by faith in Jesus Christ.

If you are Living in Abuse

It is not God's will for you to live in any type of abusive relationship. There should be no verbal abuse, physical abuse, sexual abuse or neglect of you. If you are experiencing any of it, get out of that place and away from those people. Don't believe the lie that you should stay in it. You must make a change. In North America, there is help for those who need temporary shelter from abuse. Don't be silent about it. Get help from your pastor or from a government agency if you don't have the money to move out on your own. Once you are out of the abuse, you can start planning your life with clear vision. It doesn't mean you don't love those people but you cannot and should not tolerate living in an abusive situation.

Those abusers are not the devil. They are wounded, twisted and deformed in their spirits. They are instruments of the devil. They need salvation, healing and deliverance themselves. The only way for them to see their need for Jesus Christ is for you to get out of there. As God starts blessing you and you start enjoying your life, you can become a positive witness to those people. Getting an education and a career or trade is essential in your becoming a success and in enjoying your life. College or University is the only way to get beyond your present situation. Set your sights on something higher than yourself and what you see as your life. Aim for a career or trade that can get you a job that earns above minimum wage. Your independence is important to giving you confidence. Begin to plan for your life in positive ways.

Don't focus on the past. Remember the good things God has done for you. Focus on them. Remember the blessings that God has given you. If you have been a Christian for one day, you can thank God for saving you. Think about the prayers He has answered and how He has directly provided for you. Thank Him for wisdom and revelation. Thank Him and as you do this, joy will spring up in your spirit. Gratitude and praise and worship releases joy in your spirit.

Psalm 77: 10 Then I said, "This is my grief;
   yet I will remember the years of the right hand of the Most High."
11 I will remember the works of the Lord;
   surely I will remember Your wonders of old.
12 I will meditate also on all Your work
   and ponder on Your mighty deeds.

Remember the works of the LORD. That means focus on what God has done for you. Be thankful for the answers to prayer. Be thankful He protects and keeps your life. Remember how God has taught you so that you understand spiritual truths from God's Word. Put your focus on God.

There was a period of my life where God blessed me so tremendously. It was several years as I was studying for Ministry. It seemed that I was winning souls really quickly. I witnessed to almost everyone I met. People were introducing me to Pastors and prophets and evangelists and teachers. I had opportunity to meet world renown preachers. It was such favour upon my life and God was using me in my gifts in talents both in service in my local church and in the community. I was living a life of uncommon favour.

Afterwards, I went through a rough season. None of the former things were in my life. It was tough. What I would do is read the scripture to myself. The same God that blessed me and highly favoured me in the past, was the same God I serve today. My joy is in the God who provides not in the provision itself. Yes, I enjoyed those years. I remember the good. I also embrace God in the present, thanking Him for what He has done for me in the past and in the present. I thank Him for the opportunities of the future. I can see the beauty of creation; I can see the beauty of Christ's love for the Church; I can see the beauty of God's covenant with Israel. It gives me encouragement. God's blessing on me is for all of my life. I focus on His promises and His character and His relationship with me through covenant.

Jeremiah 29: 11 For I know the plans that I have for you, says the Lord, plans for peace and not for evil, to give you a future and a hope.

Reading God's Word

Pray for understanding before you read God's Word and as you read it so that God the Holy Spirit might teach you through the Word. Get as much Word of god in you as possible to build yourself up spiritually. Apply the Scriptures in your life each day. As you are reading promises of God, include yourself as a recipient because we inherit the promises of God through our faith in Jesus Christ. The Bible is God's plan for people on earth. It directly applies to you. Claim it for yourself. Get a translation of the Bible that is best for you. I like King James because that is the scripture I mostly memorized but there are other popular versions such as the Living Bible, The New International Bible and the Modern English Version. The Amplified Bible is an excellent study Bible because it includes a literal translation of the scriptures. As you are reading the scripture, thank God for it and let your spirit be in agreement with the scriptures so you say within your spirit "Thank you God. I receive it for my life."

Apply the scriptures to your past. Let God's Word be the prominent memory you think of. Apply the Word of God in your present. Set your hope in God and his word. Let the scriptures help you to chart a course for the future. Read and study the scriptures believing for the promises to manifest in your own life. God wants you to enjoy your life today. God wants you to be blessed with all things that you might have need of in your life. Read Deuteronomy 28 and see the kind of life God promised to Moses and Israel if they obeyed the commandments of God.

Deuteronomy 28: 2 And all these blessings will come on you and overtake you if you listen to the voice of the Lord your God.

3 You will be blessed in the city and blessed in the field.

4 Your offspring will be blessed, and the produce of your ground, and the offspring of your livestock, the increase of your herd and the flocks of your sheep.

5 Your basket and your kneading bowl will be blessed.

6 You will be blessed when you come in and blessed when you go out.

7 The Lord will cause your enemies who rise up against you to be defeated before you; they will come out against you one way and flee before you seven ways.

8 The Lord will command the blessing on you in your barns and in all that you set your hand to do, and He will bless you in the land which the Lord your God is giving you.

We inherit these promises of God through our faith in Jesus Christ. It is right for you to expect the blessings of God if you are living your life as unto Him. You can read the scriptures allowed and thank God, they apply to your life. Claim them. We have an inheritance that is more than being saved so we can get to heaven. Yes, it is essential and it is important to know we are saved and will go to heaven. God though wants us to live in the Spirit on earth so that we might have the days of heaven on earth. God's blessings are also so that you may enjoy your life on earth.

Deuteronomy 11: 21 so that your days and the days of your children may be multiplied in the land which the Lord swore to your fathers to give them, as long as the days of heaven on the earth.

God wants you to see the beauty of life around you. God wants to bless you now not just in the life after this one. It is so good that people might not believe it. The God who gave His life to save your soul wants you to live in your spirit and enjoy the things of life sharing and giving and learning and sowing into others, as long as you live.

Creation

God could have made things on earth so they were dull – all grey. However, God made every creature to be beautiful. God made the sunrise to inspire and the moon to shine in magnificence and multi colour flowers and plants, trees and bushes. Oceans, forest, mountains hills, the stars in the sky – all of these things testify that God is a creative, awesome creator. God made each person unique with positive aspects and qualities that no other person has. God wants us to be inspired and awed by the beauty and majesty of creation. He did it with the purpose of giving His best to us. God gave us His best. He gives us His best. Our focus should be with thanksgiving and worship and reverence.

Pray that you will be able to see the beauty and awesomeness around you in creation and in people. Develop a heart that can see beauty and thank God for it. Gratitude is an attitude enhancer. It causes you to be joyful no matter what. God can give that type of heart. Make a decision that "I will bless the LORD" no matter what your day is like. It is a will decision. Purpose within yourself that you will praise your God. Thank God for His blessings towards you. Praise Him because He is your God.

Psalm 103: 1 Bless the Lord, O my soul,
    and all that is within me, bless His holy name.
2 Bless the Lord, O my soul,
    and forget not all His benefits,

Your soul is your mind, your will and your emotions. Praise God with all of you. We should be living in the spirit – by the infilling of the Holy Spirit. Our spirit should be leading us so that the mind, will and emotions align with God's Word. Live in the spirit – not in the soul. Literally make a spirit led decision to bless the Lord. Literally, start praising and worshipping God. As you are praising and worshipping God, you will be aligning yourself with the Word of God so that faith might be released in your life to receive God's best treasures for you in the present.

King David

David was anointed by God to be the king. Before he was made the king, he had many years running from Saul who was trying to kill him because of his jealousy of the anointing on David's life. David knew what it was like to be falsely accused and hunted by the king and his army even though David had never sinned against Saul or anyone else. The real enemy was the devil possessing Saul to hate and want to kill David. There were opportunities that David had to kill Saul. In Saul's tracking and hunting for David, he left himself vulnerable more than once. David's own men tried to tell David to kill him, but David would not kill Saul because he knew God had made him king.

Things you can do if you are being unjustly treated

1.   Sow financially into ministries that preach and teach salvation, healing, deliverance etc. Doing this attacks the devil.

2.   Sow scripture into people's lives. It causes God's Word to be honoured and releases faith in people's hearts. Angels go to bring God's Word to come to pass.

3.   Start preaching to people you meet so that more people would be saved. This renewed commitment of yours to win souls is like cutting the head off the enemy.

4.   Commit yourself wholly to God. Keep a positive attitude. Keep giving and doing your best.

David had been living amongst his enemies the Philistines, pretending to be fighting with them against Israel. What he did though is he attacked the enemy and fought for God, for Israel. He was living in a place Ziglag. While he was gone fighting, the enemy raided the town and took all David's and his men's wives and children and possessions, Al the men were crying and blaming David for it. David had nothing to do with it but often when people are hurt they blame their leaders. The men even talked about killing David.

1 Samuel 30: 6 David was greatly distressed, for the people talked of stoning him, because all the people were bitter in spirit, each over his sons and daughters. But David encouraged himself in the Lord his God.

Even though no one else was there to encourage David, David encouraged himself in the LORD. He sought God's presence. He asked God if they should go after the enemy and God confirmed to him, Yes, go and recover all. God encouraged David because David sought God first. God was his source of strength.

Chris A. Legebow

Encourage Yourself by Sowing Thanksgiving

If you do not keep a prayer journal, I would highly recommend that you do. In it you should express answers to prayers as well as scriptures God is speaking to you. I once read in Christian Life magazine a special exhortation to write a thank you note to God each day for something, including joys as well as direct answers to prayer. The magazine article recommended that at Thanksgiving, read all these thank you comments to God and thank Him for them. I started doing it. For several years, I did it. This is a specific way of getting to thank God for what He has done for us. It is good to remind ourselves of what God has done throughout the year specifically.

Thank God for the teaching and preaching you've received. Thank God for the teachers and pastors you've been privileged to receive from. If you have been a Christian for very long, God will transform your life through the preaching and teaching you receive. The Word of God will give you wisdom, insight and knowledge. We should be continuously thanking God. He gives us life and provides for us and protects us.

While you are thanking and praising God, no self-pity, no doubt, no unbelief can enter in. Your attitude of thanksgiving and gratitude gets you living with God in the present enjoying your life. Offer yourself as a living sacrifice to God each day. Ask Him to fill you and use you.

Romans 12: 1 I urge you therefore, brothers, by the mercies of God, that you present your bodies as a living sacrifice, holy, and acceptable to God, which is your reasonable service of worship. 2 Do not be conformed to this world, but be transformed by the renewing of your mind, that you may prove what is the good and acceptable and perfect will of God.

Build yourself Up

You can keep offering your life to God each day. By doing this you welcome the Holy Spirit to lead you and direct you. You can make a difference with your life. You can win some souls. You can encourage, build up and edify others. You can make a difference for God's kingdom by your offering of yourself. Give yourself to building up yourself spiritually each day. Read Christian books; listen to Christian CDs or watch Christian teaching and preaching, Build up yourself spiritually on purpose. Invest in yourself spiritually; instead of watching secular TV, put Christian preaching on. Instead of hanging out with people who don't believe the same as you. Include only believers who share the same faith.

3 BUILDING UP YOURSELF

Building yourself up in the most Holy faith

Jude 1: 20 But you, beloved, build yourselves up in your most holy faith. Pray in the Holy Spirit. 21 Keep yourselves in the love of God while you are waiting for the mercy of our Lord Jesus Christ, which leads to eternal life.

The Apostle Paul is encouraging us to build up ourselves in the most Holy faith.

Relationships

Building yourself up in the faith directly involves your relationship with God. You have got to give yourself to prayer if you want to develop relationship with God. Prayer is talking to God and listening to God. If prayer seems more of a task to you rather than a joy, you are not really communicating with God. Speaking with God means His presence is with you and in you mightily. God's presence brings joy, peace, excitement and fascination. God's presence is so awesome, it releases the Holy Spirit within us to leap and rejoice. God's presence is the most unique aspect that distinguishes Christian prayer from other faiths. Our God is alive and He lives within us. As we commune with Him tremendous life flows from our innermost being.

Don't just be content to say prayers believing you are doing some kind of religious duty. Honouring God is important certainly, but prayer releases joy. Prayer releases the manifest presence of God in the believer. If you are not feeling the presence of God, it doesn't mean He isn't listening, but it may mean you are not enjoying the privileges of being a Christian. Adam and Eve lost the presence of God because of their sin. Animal sacrifices had to be made to cover our sin so God could communicate with us at all; God is Holy; He hates sin.

A duty is something you do but don't necessarily enjoy, although I believe you can train yourself to like and enjoy every day duties. Some people prayer books of prayer. Some people pray the LORD's prayer. It is important to enter into prayer in a respectful manner. Normally, prayer should start with thanksgiving and praise. Start thanking God for your salvation. Keep thanking Him for His provision of you and protection etc. Praise God for who He is. He is mighty. He is Holy. He is Omnipotent, yet He enjoys our companionship. As you thank God and give Him praise, you will not be self-absorbed. You will be focused on God and joy will spring up out of your spirit.

Psalm 100:4 Enter into His gates with thanksgiving,
   and into His courts with praise;
   be thankful to Him, and bless His name.

Should you enter prayer in this way, God's presence always comes. He inhabits the praises of His people. After you have thanked Him and praised Him, make your petitions known to Him. That is ask Him for things you need. He delights in blessing His children. It gives God joy to give us the desires of our heart. Please don't just stop there. Also pray over yourself scriptures. Ask God to refresh you, to teach you and to guide you. Expect that He will.

Listen to what God has to say to you. Literally say, God speak to me, teach me, instruct me. God will. You must listen and as you are listening you could be completely silent or in reverent worship. It is during this experience of receiving from God where you should be most obedient. God will only give you the best of what He has for you. He will teach you, lead you and instruct you. It is by talking to and listening to God where we are transformed. God gives us a heavenly perspective of the matters of my life. We freely enter into God's presence and have the freedom to approach God without fear or shame, because of the blood of Jesus Christ. Mostly God speaks to us through Scripture. But He may speak a word or a phrase to you. He may give you a vision or an idea. God will speak to us Spirit to spirit.

John 4: 23 Yet the hour is coming, and is now here, when the true worshippers will worship the Father in spirit and truth. For the Father seeks such to worship Him. 24 God is Spirit, and those who worship Him must worship Him in spirit and truth."

Praying from Authority

As Christians, we are not saying prayers that go up to God. It's not that we hope God hears us. We live in Jesus Christ. Jesus Christ is seated on the Throne in heaven. As we pray, we pray from within Christ. We are in His presence in the Holy of Holies. As soon as we pray, the answer is on the way to us. God certainly hears us. God certainly receives a true faith prayer. That means our prayers should align with the Word of God. You can't be praying for something directly against God's will and expect to receive it. God makes clear to us the things He likes and the things He doesn't like in His commandments.

I didn't fully understand this truth until I heard Kenneth Copeland preach it. He described it as Jesus Christ comes to live in our spirit man through the person of the Holy Spirit, after we make Him our Saviour and LORD. Christ is living in us. We are also in Christ. He calls us the Body of Christ. We are members of the Body of Christ. That means we are in Christ. Jesus Christ is in the Throne room; we live in Him so we are in Him. Pray with boldness from the place of authority within Jesus Christ the resurrected LORD.

Ephesians 1: 18 that the eyes of your understanding may be enlightened, that you may know what is the hope of His calling and what are the riches of the glory of His inheritance among the saints, 19 and what is the surpassing greatness of His power toward us who believe, according to the working of His mighty power, 20 which He performed in Christ when He raised Him from the dead and seated Him at His own right hand in the heavenly places, 21 far above all principalities, and power, and might, and dominion, and every name that is named, not only in this age but also in that which is to come. 22 And He put all things. in subjection under His feet and made Him the head over all things for the church, 23 which is His body, the fullness of Him who fills all things in all ways.

Ephesians 2: 4 But God, being rich in mercy, because of His great love with which He loved us, 5 even when we were dead in sins, made us alive together with Christ (by grace you have been saved), 6 and He raised us up and seated us together in the heavenly places in Christ Jesus,

Jesus is seated in glory and it is from this place within the Holy of Holies that God. Not only is He there to hear your prayers but He is praying for us. He is making intercession for us. That means He is praying with us and for us. That should give us some boldness and some faith. Even if you do not have a prayer partner on earth near you, Jesus is praying in agreement with you.

Hebrews 7: 25 Therefore He is able to save to the uttermost those who come to God through Him, because He at all times lives to make intercession for them

Even in the book of Daniel, Daniel is praying and praying and doesn't get an answer so he continues to fast and pray for 21 days. The angel who comes to him says that God heard his prayer the moment He prayed it but he had to fight to get the prayer answer to him. There were evil spirits that tried to stop the answer to prayer, but because Daniel persisted in prayer, he received his answer. Michael the archangel came to assist the messenger angel in getting the answer to prayer to Daniel. Please know this was before Jesus died on the cross. This is before the new covenant. There is still opposition to us – but we pray with boldness knowing Jesus blood gives us entrance into God's presence.

Building up yourself

Building up yourself spiritually is always God's will for you. God wants you to be spiritually strong. If you build up your spirit man, your soul will prosper. Your body will be at optimum ability. God will prosper us spirit, soul and body. Building up yourself spiritually means feeding your spirit rather than just your mind, will and emotions. You must feed your spirit, the Word of God. You must feed your spirit by praising and worshipping God and being in God's presence. To feed your spirit, you must be with people of like precious faith. If the people are negative or not of the same faith, cut them out of your life while you are building yourself up or do the minimum you must do with them.

Church

Church should be a place where you are spiritually fed and nourished with God's Word. The preacher's words should encourage, uplift and exhort you. The function of the Body of Christ gathering together in worship and praise is a dynamic that goes beyond human words. God's presence is upon the local churches that gather in a special way; His corporate blessing and presence is manifest in the church. Different people will be motivated differently; some will prophesy; some will read scriptures; some will speak in tongues; others will interpret tongues. I am talking about God's flowing through the church body. The Body of Christ gathers to worship God and to celebrate the sacraments together and to hear the Word of God. The Holy Spirit will manifest the gifts of the Spirit in the service if we would believe and give room for it. It may mean waiting on God and not rushing after praise and worship.

1 Corinthians 14: 26 How is it then, brothers? When you come together, every one of you has a psalm, a teaching, a tongue, a revelation, and an interpretation. Let all things be done for edification.

Give no place to the devil

It is important that we have nothing that is unpleasing to God in our home or possession. I learned this the day after I had become a Christian. One day things that were important to me and that I had spent hundreds of dollars on were okay to me. The day after I got saved, The Holy Spirit got me house cleaning. Literally the spirit was prompting me to get rid of books, records and other things that were not pleasing to God. Any image of any false God must get thrown out. Anything of the occult or pornography or illegal or against God in any way must get thrown out. You will know it because God will tug at your heart and speak to you to get rid of it. It will be a strong prompting in the inner man that moves you to get rid of it.

Ephesians 4: 27 Do not give place to the devil.

This is particularly important if you are in need of encouragement or an answer from God. You should cut out unnecessary TV and entertainment. Only let your eyes see what is pure; only listen to that which will build you up. Have no token of any other religion or anything unpleasing to God. Keeping those types of things is an entrance point for the enemy – the devil. Give no entrance point for the devil. If you are wondering if you should keep it, get rid of it. If you 're not sure,' get rid of it. There should not be anything that is unpleasing in any way to God. Make a serious decision to press into God cutting off anything unpleasing to Him. Your human will has to do with it. You must hate sin and love God. You must choose God for yourself over anything else.

Knowing Jesus is LORD

I know people who know that Jesus died for their sins but who live on earth in a meagre existence. They lived addicted to cigarettes or alcohol or drugs or sexual immorality. They become addicts to pleasures of the flesh that do not satisfy a person. I'm saying there is a life on earth we are to be living, the high calling of God in Christ Jesus (Philippians 3: 14). There is a way we can live Holy lives on the earth. It is not keeping a list of I can'ts. Some people are religious and they try to use their human will power to obey God. They make up a list of I can't do this or that. That is not living the Christian life. Living a life in freedom of worship to God involves total acceptance of God in all parts of your life. It means you surrender all. As you give yourself to God completely, you want to please God. You want to serve God. You realize He only wants the best for you so you choose Him.

Free Will

In the Old Testament, a slave would serve a master for six years and then be set free. What would happen though is sometimes the slaves realized the life they had with their master was good. Perhaps they married and had children. They did not want to start life alone. They wanted to stay serving their master. I know it sounds hard to believe because we live in Western Culture where slavery is very negative. The truth is there have been good masters and terrible masters. I would always choose freedom. Most of us would.

I realized though, after living for God only a couple of weeks, that His life and the goodness and mercy He had shown to me was beyond what my old self could have imagined. I am free; I do not have to serve God. Jesus set me free. I can go anywhere and do anything. I realize the best possible life for me is living in Christ and living for Christ. My pierced ears are a reminder to me that I willingly serve the LORD Jesus Christ. Just as the slave had a pierced ear, choosing to stay with his or her master, I choose to live for God.

Deuteronomy 15: 16 It shall be, if he says to you, "I will not go away from you," because he loves you and your house, because he is well off with you, 17 then you must take an awl and pierce it through his ear into the door, and he shall be your servant forever. And you shall also do likewise to your female servant.

JESUS IS LORD

I know that I do not have to be addicted to anything. Jesus Christ set me free from the bondages of sin. Jesus Christ gave me life with such joy, laughter, peace and fulfillment, I know that I know living with Jesus is the best for me. I know it because for 35 years He has been faithful to me, provided for me, delivered me, healed me and keeps me. God has got our best interests in heart. He gave us His son Jesus because God wanted to restore communion with mankind. God wanted us to be able to speak with Him and have communion with Him as Adam and Eve once had before they sinned.

In Christ, you don't simply cease from sin. You replace it with God's Word. Study the Word of God. Take a Bible class. Watch Christian Media. Do something to build up your inner man in faith. You replace it with serving God and being a member of the body of Christ on earth. You give to people. You care. You bring joy to people. You have a strong testimony to share of how Christ has delivered you. You do not have to be in any type of addiction. If you truly are a Christian, you will hate sin. You will not want to do it. You don't have to live with it. You can be set free.

Giving your all

If you do not know God as Saviour, Healer and deliverer, you've got to get some word in you. You have got to get to a church that teaches and preaches the literal Word of God as being for your life. If you haven't been filled with the Holy Spirit, you should pray for it. God promises it to us who would believe. If you have strayed away from God, repent and return to God. First it is an inward tug at your heart. Pray and let God satisfy you with His Spirit. Examine your heart. If there is anything not right, make it right by praying and asking Jesus to cleanse you and wash you in His blood. If you have truly pressed into God and surrendered all, you can rejoice because God has got the best possible life for you. As you encourage yourself in God, Ask God to refresh you and let the high praises of God flow from your innermost being.

There is a high way to live; it is the way of living Holy in God's presence. It will bring you such joy that it is hard to express with only words.

Isaiah 35: 8 A highway shall be there, a roadway,
    and it shall be called the Highway of Holiness.

Church

Church is to be a gathering of saints who believe the same. I can remember being in church when I could barely wait to get into the next service. People would be healed. Demons would be cast out. People would use the gifts of the spirit. The Word of God was exactly what I needed to hear. A Church filled with the Spirit of God honours God first. You may not know what is going to happen from week to week because God flows in supernatural ways and people obey the promptings of the Holy Spirit. If you don't go to a church where you know they believe in salvation, healing and deliverance, you are not in the right church. It may be a temporary place for you; you can supplement your life with Christian Media. Please know though, there are Holy Spirit filled Churches that preach and teach God's word and that flow in the Holy Spirit. That is the type of place a Christian can thrive, learn and contribute.

True Christian friends

There are true Christian friends that you can share the secrets of your heart with who will pray for you and with you. They want God's best for you. They care about you spiritually. They won't be content to just know about the events of your life. They will want to know how you are doing spiritually. If you do not presently have these types of friends in your life. Pray for them. Pray 'O God join me together with people of like precious faith.' You can get excellent support from Christian Media and faith based TV. They will pray for you. I thank God for them; I also thank God for my close Christian friends who care about me spiritually.

I thank God for their prayers and our talks about God and our sharing of the sacraments, ministry together and deep friendship that is because of Jesus Christ. God has always given me somebody. Sometimes they were not in my life much. Sometimes, I only saw them at church. Sometimes, I only see them rarely because of different schedule. I know those people love me and care for me spiritually. It's kinda' like if you had a good parent, you were comforted by him or her and that parent always cared for your best interests. God can give you true Christian friends who care for you spiritually. If you are the first Christian in your family, pray for other Christians friends who share your passion for Christ. These types of friendships are so precious because they are first spiritual and then natural.

Your friends

If your non- Christian friends want you to partake in sinful activities, if they want you to compromise your faith in any way, have nothing to do with them. It may mean that you are alone for a period. True friends want you to be joyful and they will respect your faith. A non-Christian can never be your best friend if you are a Christian because you are not equally yoked. A yoke used to be a piece of wood or metal that joined two donkeys or two oxen so they could pull together as a team. They were used in farming and for labour. You could not yoke a donkey with an ox because they don't walk the same. They don't act the same. They are not the same.

2 Corinthians 6: 14 Do not be unequally yoked together with unbelievers. For what fellowship has righteousness with unrighteousness? What communion has light with darkness? 15 What agreement has Christ with Belial? Or what part has he who believes with an unbeliever?

Alignments

If you need encouragement, cut out unessential people or people who do not add to you spiritually. Align yourself with the right alignments. Who you align with matters. In global context, nations align themselves with other nations. They create pacts and peace treaties and trade agreements. These alliances are important to all aspects of intercultural exchange. If there is any breach of trust, the nations impose sanctions on nations that do not keep their word. An example would be someone killing a citizen of the allied nation. That nation could restrict access to the offender. That nation would not be able to trade or send people freely etc. It is considered very important by nations. Allies matter. God cares particularly who aligns with Israel because He has a special plan for Israel and will one day return to earth to rule from Jerusalem.

God also cares who you align with and who aligns with you. You should align with people who believe the same. An example is that I have often mentioned preachers in my books who have impacted my life and from whom I obtained truth. I don't say their names for any other reason than I believe they helped me truly and can add value to your life as well. Aligning with people of faith has a cost to it. I mean that should you align with Spirit filled Charismatic Pentecostal people, others will term you as radical. They said the same thing about Jesus early disciples and apostles. They were known as the radical people of the way. They were the followers of the Christ. Not everyone likes us but they know who we are. This passage in acts shows that their reputation was known.

Acts 17: 6 But when they did not find them, they dragged Jason and some brothers to the city officials, crying out, "These men who have turned the world upside down have come here also,

Those people who noticed the Christians feared them and didn't want Jesus Christ coming in and changing any part of their lives. Christ can totally transform a people. Certainly, the idols would be crushed and no idols would be bought by Christians. That would lose the idol creating business quite a bit of money. That same type of fear exists with some people about Jesus Christ.

If you are a New Christian

Start praying at least 15 minutes a day. Thank Him, Praise Him, give your Petitions, worship Him. Give yourself to God first. Ask God to give you discerning of spirits strong. Ask God to give you wisdom and words of wisdom. Start praying over yourself the promises of God in Scripture.

Baptism of The Holy Spirit

If you are not baptized in the Holy Spirit, you can be. Start praying and asking God for the baptism of the Holy Spirit. The same Spirit that raised up Jesus from the dead can dwell in you and quicken your mortal body (Romans 8: 11). The Holy Spirit in you is the manifest presence of God in you.

If you have been baptized in the Holy Spirit, don't believe that is all there is to it. There is more. God wants to use you in the gifts of the Spirit. God wants to teach you to pray in the spirit so He can pray with you, in you and through you. You've been given a gift to use to win souls and to minister as a living witness for Christ. The anointing of the Holy Spirit can break strongholds from off of people; you can see people saved, healed and set free to worship God. Once you are baptized in the Spirit, pray in tongues. If you need a miracle, walk around or kneel and pray in tongues. Let God pray through you. Praise God in tongues. Pray in tongues. God will be praying and praising through you. It will strengthen and encourage your spirit.

Romans 8: 26 Likewise, the Spirit helps us in our weaknesses, for we do not know what to pray for as we ought, but the Spirit Himself intercedes for us with groanings too deep for words. 27 He who searches the hearts knows what the mind of the Spirit is, because He intercedes for the saints according to the will of God.

Praying In Tongues

Praying and praising in tongues is a way of stirring up faith in your spirit. As you are praying and praising in tongues, the Holy Spirit is praying through you and for you, the perfect will of God concerning you and the situations you are praying for. Rather than you making a request or a petition, they are excellent but if you need to encourage yourself, they are not the best way. The most direct way is the best way – go to the source. Stir up yourself in the Spirit. Literally say it out loud:" I stir up myself in the spirit of God" and as you do, your soul must obey your spirit. The Holy Spirit will come and refresh you.

The Holy Spirit will pray for you. The Holy Spirit may or may not reveal to you in English the things you were praying for. Example, If I want to send a brief encouraging message to someone, I may send an email or a text. I may send a letter or a card. I may phone the person directly. They are all acceptable forms of communication. Instead of me wondering what to say, the Holy Spirit gives me the exact message I should give (in tongues) that would be the best possible encouragement to the friend.

The Holy Spirit would choose the medium for it. Example, rather than me choosing a way of communication, the Holy Spirit would release the word to my spirit. It would be strong and the most excellent because He is God and He gives the best possible way and the best possible Word. Sometimes, I have prayed for people and the Holy Spirit would translate into English the things I was praying. Often it was scripture. I would take the Words and find the scriptures in the Bible and write them in a card or letter and send them to the person God was directing me to pray for. It was a Word of encouragement that only God could bring.

As I pray in tongues for myself, as I stir up the gifts, sometimes God gives me the interpretation of tongues and I will find the scripture and write it in my prayer journal. Often God gives me the direct answer to what is necessary in my life by giving me His Word. It strengthens me, builds me up and encourages me. I keep a record of these scriptures and pray them and confess them mixed with faith. God's Word released with faith always produces results.

Christian Worship

If you don't know any Christian songs, write some of the titles of songs in Church. Type them into the Internet. Get the words to the songs so you can sing them at home during your worship. Get some Christian music in your life. Don't listen to profanity or songs that release negative words or feelings. There is every type of Christian music. There is jazz, pop, rock, alternative, classical etc. Get Christian music in your life. Listen to something that will be building you up and strengthening you.

Christian Movies and Entertainment

Get some Christian movies in your life. There are excellent Christian movies with strong Christian values that you can rent or purchase. These movies will truly be family rated. They are approved by Hallmark and Dove Approval. If you don't have a bookstore at church, go to the one in town. If you can't find one, type Christian movies into the Internet and shop on line. There are hundreds of family friendly, faith based movies.

It is not that you cannot take part in secular music and movies. Some of them are wholesome and family rated. If you know you are need of encouragement – don't partake in secular, ungodly music or movies. Pretend that Jesus is physically accompanying you to the movie or music. The things you are partaking of should be something you have no embarrassment about.

The truth is the Holy Spirit is in you wherever you go. You should not take part of anything that would cause you to be ashamed or that would be ungodly. How do you know? Only the Holy Spirit can direct you in this. If you truly pray, Holy Spirit let me know if there is anything unpleasing to God – He will. It is not a religious thing. It is a matter of the spiritual origin or roots of the music or movies. Judge the source of the movie or music or entertainment by its fruit.

Luke 6: 43 "A good tree does not bear corrupt fruit, nor does a corrupt tree bear good fruit. 44 Each tree is known by its own fruit. Men do not gather figs from thorns, nor do they gather grapes from a wild bush.

The fruit of music or movies or entertainment has a spiritual origin. The Bible gives us an example of some of the fruit and the origin. If the entertainment has any of the fruit of the flesh in it but you still like it, you should pray and ask God to soften your heart and to lead your life. God hates sin. If you choose things of the flesh to feed yourself, you will not reap a spiritually abundant harvest. If you sow to the flesh, you will reap of the flesh. If you choose the fruits of righteousness, and you delight in them, you will be directly feeding your spirit man. You will be encouraging yourself in God; you will reap encouragement and strength in your spirit.

Galatians 5: 19 Now the works of the flesh are revealed, which are these: adultery, sexual immorality, impurity, lewdness, 20 idolatry, sorcery, hatred, strife, jealousy, rage, selfishness, dissensions, heresies, 21 envy, murders, drunkenness, carousing, and the like. I warn you, as I previously warned you, that those who do such things shall not inherit the kingdom of God.

22 But the fruit of the Spirit is love, joy, peace, patience, gentleness, goodness, faith, 23 meekness, and self-control; against such there is no law. 24 Those who are Christ's have crucified the flesh with its passions and lusts. 25 If we live in the Spirit, let us also walk in the Spirit. 26 Let us not be conceited, provoking one another and envying one another.

Increase Your Presence O God

In the last decade. there was a revival in International House of prayer

Kansas City, Missouri. There were people saved, healed delivered. I noticed a reoccurring prayer: "Increase your presence O God". What that means is God let me decrease while you increase in my life. It doesn't mean God is going to change but that you are yielding yourself to God so that God might fill you and transform you by His presence from glory to glory (2 Corinthians 3: 18).

Pray yielding yourself to God in this way, giving yourself wholly to God and as you do, His presence will increase mightily in you and you will be strengthened with might in your inner man. Pray O let God be magnified in me; Let Jesus Christ be glorified in me. These types of personal surrender prayers get you in the Spirit and sowing to the spirit that you might reap of the Holy Spirit. As a magnifying glass magnifies words on a page, set your spirit to magnify Jesus Christ while you live on the earth. Let Christ be magnified in you that God might be glorified through your life. As God is magnified in you, you are going to feel His presence. God is not a feeling but His manifest presence will most certainly be felt. You will realize God is present with you in a strong way. It will cause you to want to praise and worship.

You can go to the prayer room in International House of Prayer through GOD TV or the Internet. There is 24 hour a day prayer and praise and worship and intercession. There are different worship leaders and different aspects all of it praise and worship and intercessory prayer 24/7/365. It is an awesome way to get yourself with people who are worshipping God directly.

Thank God by Faith

If you don't feel it immediately, you pray and praise by faith in God's word that says God inhabits the praises of His people. Say "God I am praising you and your word says that you inhabit the praises of your people. I thank you for your presence, your Holy presence." As you pray or praise in faith, expect God to show up strong because He will honour your faith.

Use God's word to pray and praise and worship. I thank God for the mighty prophet Kelly Varner, who I have been privileged to hear and receive form. He was talking about giving yourself to praise and worship and spoke that praising God and worshipping God with God's Word was mighty because it was directly to God the source. He gave a special blessing to our praise and worship leader and said what he liked about her was that she was not leading the people to talk or sing at God but by using God's word directly speaking and praising God with His Word as the emphasis.

If you are not enjoying worshipping God, get yourself some different music. Praise and worship manifests God's presence more pleasurable than any other pleasure of the earth. Get yourself Spirit filled music and praise and worship so that you see how awesome it is to worship God and praise Him. Give yourself wholly to God: Holy to God. Let the Holy Spirit inspire you to praise and worship. As you do, God's presence comes strong. You will begin to see all the things of earth from a heavenly perspective as you focus on God who is mighty.

No matter what your age is – give your all to Jesus

Some people believe they are too old for God to use the, Others believe they are too young. God can use a child. God can use you no matter what your age is if you give yourself to Him wholly. The first year I got saved, there was a man in my Bible class who was in his 80's. He didn't come to the LORD until his 80's but he was passionate about God and used to drive more than an hour to attend that Bible class because he wanted all of God that he could get. He was giving his whole being to God. He was witnessing to people. God renewed him and after praise and worship there was a glow about him as God's presence was mightily upon him. Pray God let me make a difference in my generation. Let me honour you with my life.

Maybe you could start a Christian club in your school or workplace. Maybe God can use you to inspire those you meet with the anointing of God on you so they will want to know the reason for your joy. Give your best even if you can't openly witness in your workplace, do something for Christ. I know a professional woman who uses Christmas as an opportunity to give to those in her secular workplace. There is always some type of Christian message. At Christmas and Easter people are more open to receive things about Jesus without being offended. You must live a life of excellence though. If you do, and you give, it may impact someone's life for eternity. You can't do everything but you can do something. Do the something you can do for the glory of God.

Pray for God's Favour

Start praying for God's favour. There are many scriptures where God promises to show His favour on His people. As you pray for God's favour, expect it. God can use you with your gifts and talents to show God's glory to all kinds of people.

Psalm 5: 12 For You, Lord, will bless the righteous;
  You surround him with favor like a shield.

Pray for favour with all kinds of people. Marilyn Hickey said she started praying and thanking God for favour and everywhere she goes with Christians and non-Christians God is giving her favour. God even opened an opportunity for her to preach in a Mosque. Joel Osteen, gets favour with all types of people. He thanks God for favour and believes for it and gets it. People see him smiling and friendly and loving them with all his being. God's favour on someone makes that person seem irresistible to others. It's that Jesus shines through the person and people see the anointing of God on them. Expect God to use you in the gifts of the Spirit. Expect God to give you favour because you are a person in blood covenant with Jehovah God.

Stir up the gifts of the Spirit within you. Especially stir up the gift of discerning of spirits so God can help you through each day with wisdom. Stirring up the gifts means you are yielding to God in all those areas. It means you are available and willing to be used of God. Expect God to use you. Literally put your hand on yourself and pray over yourself saying out loud ' I stir…" name the gifts. You are stirring up your spirit to be released to do God's will. What you are doing is aligning yourself with God's Word directly. You are giving yourself to be used by God.

1 Corinthians 12: 7 But the manifestation of the Spirit is given to everyone for the common good. 8 To one is given by the Spirit the word of wisdom, to another the word of knowledge by the same Spirit, 9 to another faith by the same Spirit, to another gifts of healings by the same Spirit, 10 to another the working of miracles, to another prophecy, to another discerning of spirits, to another various kinds of tongues, and to another the interpretation of tongues. 11 But that one and very same Spirit works all these, dividing to each one individually as He will.

Start Sowing to the Spirit

Get on the Internet

Even if you cannot physically go preach the gospel to people, you can preach to them using other means. You can write cards to people encouraging them with scriptures. You can sow God's Word into people by buying them CD's or Books. You can post a blog on the Internet.

Start a Blog. You could write a blog and post it to your Facebook account. If you don't know what I'm talking about, get someone to show you how to use a computer and the Internet and start preaching Christ through the Internet. It's also a good way to keep up with your family members and friends.

Keeping a journal is an excellent way to document your day and also the things you are thinking about and scriptures that God is speaking to you. This task you mostly do for yourself but as you reflect to write, God may give you words to encourage others by. Start journaling the people you meet and places you go etc. as if your life matters because it does matter.

Do what you can do

Maybe you can't go door to door preaching or volunteer at Church for whatever the reason; you can do something though. Do what you can do and expect God to use you. Stir up the gifts of the Spirit. Submit to God. Give of your finances. Sow spiritually into others. Do something to share Christ. Get access to the Internet so you can get excellent teaching and preaching. Post a blog. Post Christian scriptures and messages on all types of social media. Do something for God on purpose sowing to the Spirit so that you might reap of the Spirit.

Expect God to honour His word. God desires to bless you and see you prosperous. God wants you to succeed. Do something each day to align yourself with God's people. Claim the blessings of the blood covenant of Jesus over yourself. Keep pressing into God. Don't be content to live off yesterday's manna. Press in each day for God to manifest His presence in your life. Contribute at least 1 hour a day to your spiritual growth. It could be praying and praising and reading God's Word and listening to preaching or reading Christian materials that will encourage you.

4 CONCLUSION

Building yourself up in the Holy Faith is boosting yourself up in the spirit man. Any sign that you need encouragement is a sign that you are in war. We don't usually see our enemy the devil and his demons; we usually only see the people they use. The truth is there is a spiritual attack on you. First you must realize it. Next you must do something about it. You have got to fight. You have got to fight with all of your being, but it is the fight of faith you must do.

1 Timothy 6: 12 Fight the good fight of faith. Lay hold on eternal life, to which you are called and have professed a good profession before many witnesses.

You must fight in the spirit man not in the flesh. You must use the spiritual weapons God has given us, not weapons of the world or weapons of the people who are against you. You must keep your heart pure and holy. Important is getting dressed first.

The Armor of God is more than an analogy. The armor of God is spiritual. You cannot fight in your own strength or even in your own faith. You must use the spiritual armour God instructs us to put on. It is Jesus Christ's righteousness not our own. It is the faith of Jesus who lives in us who empowers us and strengthens us.

Romans 3: 21 But now, apart from the law, the righteousness of God is revealed, being witnessed by the Law and the Prophets. 22 This righteousness of God comes through faith in Jesus Christ[k] to all and upon all who believe, for there is no distinction.

Knowing you are right with God and can approach the throne of God's grace gives you boldness. You realize God is on your side. He is more awesome and mightier than anything you could be facing.

Encouraging yourself in the LORD

God will often send people to encourage you and to give you words or phrases that inspire faith. Often your pastor or a minister from Christian media is used to speak the exact words you need to hear. I would compare this to God providing for Israel in the desert as they wandered for forty years. He supplied manna and water and even quail. God will send provisions but you must also strengthen yourself.

To encourage yourself in the LORD is necessary. You must get spiritual food into your spirit. You must cut out unnecessary entertainment and activities while you are in need of encouragement. Give yourself to God wholly. Read the Word of God. Pray in the spirit, in tongues and in English. Pray longer than usual in tongues. Read the word of God. Find scriptures that will build up your spirit.

There are some scriptures included in a chapter in this book. You may use an online concordance or a book of scriptures ordered by topics to get others. Read the word out loud. Pray the word. Confess the word with faith. You are speaking with your mouth the answers to your prayer. You are prophetically speaking over your life. Let it be with boldness and faith, knowing that God releases angels to bring about the scriptures you speak. Your words are going into your own spirit but they are words going into the atmosphere also. The demons tremble if a Christian is praying in faith God's Word. You are aligning yourself with God's Word.

Build up yourself

To Build up yourself in the Holy Faith is important. It can only occur through prayer, worship, praise, reading God's word prayerfully. Input Christian teaching and teaching into your life directly through excellent faith filled Bible teachers and preachers from the Internet or Tv or Satellite. Get the Word of God on the inside of you. I don't just mean any word. Find the scriptures that directly relate to your spiritual situation. God will send a message to you through the Word of God as you are prayerfully reading. He can also use tv preachers, or your Christian friends. He may use your pastor. He may use your own spirit as you are praying in tongues, God may give you the interpretation of tongues and it could be a scripture or direct answer to your situation. God's word can radically transform your life. Praying that RHEMA word is important because you are coming into direct agreement with what God says. It means no enemy can stand against you.

There are excellent resources that can strengthen you and equip you to build yourself up spiritually. Some are mentioned in my book. Please connect with Christians for additional prayer. It can come from your family or friends or local church or TV ministries that pray in faith for their partners. Prayer will release angels to protect you and to bring about God's will for you which is victory. God wants you to be whole. God's pleasure is in your victory and in giving you the desires of your heart. Please read through the prayers included. If you have not been baptized in the Holy Spirit. It is essential for you to receive this gift promised by God to all who would believe on Jesus Christ. The baptism of the Holy Spirit releases power to pray in tongues, to minister the gospel and to be more closely attuned to the Holy Spirit's promptings in your life. You must live in the spirit and from your spirit man. You must feed your spirit man. You must strengthen your spirit man by prayer and the Word of God.

Please read through the scriptures included in this book. It is only a brief topical selection of scriptures I believe are related to the topic of this book. As you read them, pray. As you pray, confess them as proclamations to God and all spirits that can hear you that you believe God's word. Literally believe that as you pray, angels are released into action to bring about the words you've prayed. Praying God's Word assures agreement with God and alignment with God.

Do not believe there is no end. God knows about your situation and cares. God is a righteous judge. Do not use carnal ways to fight your fight. It is only by the Holy Spirit filling your spirit that you will stand and overcome. God is a righteous judge. He will fight for you. Let the angels be released to go fight against the enemy of your soul. Proclaim God's Word. Be assured, God knows what is occurring and He will keep His covenant with you.

Luke 18: 7 And shall not God avenge His own elect and be patient with them, who cry day and night to Him? 8 I tell you, He will avenge them speedily. Nevertheless, when the Son of Man comes, will He find faith on the earth?"

2 Thessalonians 1: 6 It is a righteous matter with God to repay with tribulation those who trouble you, 7 and to give you who are troubled rest with us when the Lord Jesus is revealed from heaven with His mighty angels, 8 in flaming fire taking vengeance on those who do not know God and do not obey the gospel of our Lord Jesus Christ. 9 They shall be punished with eternal destruction, isolated from the presence of the Lord and from the glory of His power, 10 when He comes, in that Day, to be glorified in His saints and to be marveled at by all those who believe, because our testimony among you was believed.

5 CLOSING PRAYERS

Prayer to accept Jesus or rededicate your life

God forgive me for my sins. I cannot please you with my own efforts. I believe Jesus, that you died for my sins, rose from the dead and have ascended into Heaven. I believe you are returning soon for your Church. I receive you as my Saviour and LORD. Thank you for your blood that cleanses me so that is it just as if I never sinned. Come, fill me with your Holy Spirit. Come teach me and instruct me, lead me and guide me. Give me connections with true Christians. Thank you for your mercy towards me. In Jesus name I pray. Amen.

Prayer for Baptism of the Holy Spirit

Jesus thank you that you are my Saviour and my Lord. Scripture says the gift of the Holy Spirit is for all those who believe on you. God I want the baptism of the Holy Spirit with the evidence of speaking in tongues. I want what your word says you will give to all who believe on you. Come, Holy Spirit fill me to overflowing with your presence. Jesus baptize me in the Holy Spirit. [begin to thank God for what He has done for you. Begin to worship God. Let the Holy Spirit pray and praise through you.]

Prayer for protection

Thank you God that your blood covers me. Jesus thank you for your blood on the mercy seat in heaven that speaks covenant with me. Thank you for angels that guard over me to protect me and that bring your word to come to pass concerning my life. Thank you that I dwell in the secret place of the most high God. Thank you that you cover me with your wing. Thank you for a hedge of protection around me. Thank you for godly people who pray for me. Thank you that you intercede and pray for me. Thank you for the angel of the LORD that hearkens to your word. Thank you for the angel of the LORD that encompasses me about. Thank you God that you fight against them that fight against me. Thank you for divine protection. I plead the blood of your covenant with me Jesus thanking you that no weapon formed against me can prosper and that every tongue that rises against me I will condemn. This is my heritage as a servant of the LORD and my righteousness is because of your precious blood Jesus. Amen.

Prayer for release of people

O God thank you for divine connections. Release people into my life who can help me that I can also help. Give me strong covenant relationships. Let me live in the Holy Spirit so I might receive your promptings and leadings with people to know if I should be giving to them or if they can help me. Thank you God for releasing people into my life. Thank you for divine favour that surrounds me like a shield. Thank you for divine connections. In Jesus name. Amen.

Prayer for release of angels

God I thank you that you are the captain of the host of Heaven. You rule and reign in glory. I pray for a release of angels to minister on my behalf who will bring your word to come to pass. Thank you for angels who will fight for me enforcing your Word. Thank you that I have that I have the victory through Jesus Christ. I pray for a release of ministering spirits, angels who will bring my prayers and confessions of faith to completion. In Jesus name. Amen.

6 SCRIPTURES

SCRIPTURES FOR VICTORY IN ALL AREAS OF LIFE

Romans 8: 37 Nay, in all these things we are more than conquerors through him that loved us.

Philippians 4: 13 I can do all things through Christ which strengtheneth me.

2 Corinthians 2: 14 Now thanks be unto God, which always causeth us to triumph in Christ, and maketh manifest the savour of his knowledge by us in every place.

Psalm 108: 13 Through God we shall do valiantly: for he it is that shall tread down our enemies.

Ps 60: 12 Through God we shall do valiantly: for he it is that shall tread down our enemies.

Jude: 20 But ye, beloved, building up yourselves on your most holy faith, praying in the Holy Ghost,

Ephesians 5: 19 Speaking to yourselves in psalms and hymns and spiritual songs, singing and making melody in your heart to the Lord;

Scriptures to Stir your Faith

Mark 10:52
And Jesus said unto him, Go thy way; thy faith hath made thee whole. And immediately he received his sight, and followed Jesus in the way.

Mark 11:22
And Jesus answering saith unto them, Have faith in God.

Luke 5:20
And when he saw their faith, he said unto him, Man, thy sins are forgiven thee.

Luke 7:9
When Jesus heard these things, he marvelled at him, and turned him about, and said unto the people that followed him, I say unto you, I have not found so great faith, no, not in Israel.

Luke 7:50
And he said to the woman, Thy faith hath saved thee; go in peace.

Luke 8:25
And he said unto them, Where is your faith? And they being afraid wondered, saying one to another, What manner of man is this! for he commandeth even the winds and water, and they obey him.

Luke 8:48
And he said unto her, Daughter, be of good comfort: thy faith hath made thee whole; go in peace.

Luke 12:28
If then God so clothe the grass, which is to day in the field, and tomorrow is cast into the oven; how much more will he clothe you, O ye of little faith?

Luke 12:42
And the Lord said, Who then is that faithful and wise steward, whom his lord shall make ruler over his household, to give them their portion of meat in due season?

Luke 16:10
He that is faithful in that which is least is faithful also in much: and he that is unjust in the least is unjust also in much.

Luke 16:11
If therefore ye have not been faithful in the unrighteous mammon, who will commit to your trust the true riches?

Luke 16:12
And if ye have not been faithful in that which is another man's, who shall give you that which is your own?

Luke 17:5
And the apostles said unto the Lord, Increase our faith.

Luke 17:6
And the Lord said, If ye had faith as a grain of mustard seed, ye might say unto this sycamine tree, Be thou plucked up by the root, and be thou planted in the sea; and it should obey you.

Luke 17:19
And he said unto him, Arise, go thy way: thy faith hath made thee whole.

Luke 18:42
And Jesus said unto him, Receive thy sight: thy faith hath saved thee.

Luke 22:32
But I have prayed for thee, that thy faith fail not: and when thou art converted, strengthen thy brethren.

John 20:27
Then saith he to Thomas, Reach hither thy finger, and behold my hands; and reach hither thy hand, and thrust it into my side: and be not faithless, but believing.

Acts 3:16
And his name through faith in his name hath made this man strong, whom ye see and know: yea, the faith which is by him hath given him this perfect soundness in the presence of you all.

Romans 4:14
For if they which are of the law be heirs, faith is made void, and the promise made of none effect:

Romans 4:16
Therefore it is of faith, that it might be by grace; to the end the promise might be sure to all the seed; not to that only which is of the law, but to that also which is of the faith of Abraham; who is the father of us all,

Romans 4:19
And being not weak in faith, he considered not his own body now dead, when he was about an hundred years old, neither yet the deadness of Sarah's womb:

Romans 4:20
He staggered not at the promise of God through unbelief; but was strong in faith, giving glory to God;

Romans 5:1
Therefore being justified by faith, we have peace with God through our Lord Jesus Christ:

Romans 5:2
By whom also we have access by faith into this grace wherein we stand, and rejoice in hope of the glory of God.

Romans 9:30
What shall we say then? That the Gentiles, which followed not after righteousness, have attained to righteousness, even the righteousness which is of faith.

Romans 10:6
But the righteousness which is of faith speaketh on this wise, Say not in thine heart, Who shall ascend into heaven? (that is, to bring Christ down from above:)

Romans 10:8
But what saith it? The word is nigh thee, even in thy mouth, and in thy heart: that is, the word of faith, which we preach;

Romans 10:17
So then faith cometh by hearing, and hearing by the word of God.

Romans 11:20
Well; because of unbelief they were broken off, and thou standest by faith. Be not high minded, but fear:

Romans 12:3
For I say, through the grace given unto me, to every man that is among you, not to think of himself more highly than he ought to think; but to think soberly, according as God hath dealt to every man the measure of faith.

Romans 12:6
Having then gifts differing according to the grace that is given to us, whether prophecy, let us prophesy according to the proportion of faith;

Romans 14:1
Him that is weak in the faith receive ye, but not to doubtful disputations.

Romans 14:23
And he that doubteth is damned if he eat, because he eateth not of faith: for whatsoever is not of faith is sin.

1 Corinthians 2:5
That your faith should not stand in the wisdom of men, but in the power of God.

1 Corinthians 4:2
Moreover it is required in stewards, that a man be found faithful.

1 Corinthians 12:9
To another faith by the same Spirit; to another the gifts of healing by the same Spirit;

1 Corinthians 13:2
And though I have the gift of prophecy, and understand all mysteries, and all knowledge; and though I have all faith, so that I could remove mountains, and have not charity, I am nothing.

1 Corinthians 13:13
And now abideth faith, hope, charity, these three; but the greatest of these is charity.

1 Corinthians 15:14
And if Christ be not risen, then is our preaching vain, and your faith is also vain.

1 Corinthians 15:17
And if Christ be not raised, your faith is vain; ye are yet in your sins.

1 Corinthians 16:13
Watch ye, stand fast in the faith, quit you like men, be strong.

2 Corinthians 1:24
Not for that we have dominion over your faith, but are helpers of your joy: for by faith ye stand.

2 Corinthians 4:13
We having the same spirit of faith, according as it is written, I believed, and therefore have I spoken; we also believe, and therefore speak;

2 Corinthians 5:7
(For we walk by faith, not by sight:)

2 Corinthians 8:7
Therefore, as ye abound in everything, in faith, and utterance, and knowledge, and in all diligence, and in your love to us, see that ye abound in this grace also.

2 Corinthians 10:15
Not boasting of things without our measure, that is, of other men's labours; but having hope, when your faith is increased, that we shall be enlarged by you according to our rule abundantly,

Galatians 2:16
Knowing that a man is not justified by the works of the law, but by the faith of Jesus Christ, even we have believed in Jesus Christ, that we might be justified by the faith of Christ, and not by the works of the law: for by the works of the law shall no flesh be justified.

Galatians 2:20
I am crucified with Christ: nevertheless I live; yet not I, but Christ liveth in me: and the life which I now live in the flesh I live by the faith of the Son of God, who loved me, and gave himself for me.

Galatians 3:2
This only would I learn of you, Received ye the Spirit by the works of the law, or by the hearing of faith?

Galatians 3:5
He therefore that ministereth to you the Spirit, and worketh miracles among you, doeth he it by the works of the law, or by the hearing of faith?

Galatians 3:7
Know ye therefore that they which are of faith, the same are the children of Abraham.

Galatians 3:8
And the scripture, foreseeing that God would justify the heathen through faith, preached before the gospel unto Abraham, saying, In thee shall all nations be blessed.

Galatians 3:9
So then they which be of faith are blessed with faithful Abraham.

Galatians 3:11
But that no man is justified by the law in the sight of God, it is evident: for, The just shall live by faith.

Galatians 3:12
And the law is not of faith: but, The man that doeth them shall live in them.

Galatians 3:14
That the blessing of Abraham might come on the Gentiles through Jesus Christ; that we might receive the promise of the Spirit through faith.

Galatians 3:22
But the scripture hath concluded all under sin, that the promise by faith of Jesus Christ might be given to them that believe.

Galatians 3:23
But before faith came, we were kept under the law, shut up unto the faith which should afterwards be revealed.

Galatians 3:24
Wherefore the law was our schoolmaster to bring us unto Christ, that we might be justified by faith.

Galatians 3:25
But after that faith is come, we are no longer under a schoolmaster.

Galatians 3:26
For ye are all the children of God by faith in Christ Jesus.

Galatians 5:5
For we through the Spirit wait for the hope of righteousness by faith.

Galatians 5:6
For in Jesus Christ neither circumcision availeth any thing, nor uncircumcision; but faith which worketh by love.

Galatians 5:22
But the fruit of the Spirit is love, joy, peace, longsuffering, gentleness, goodness, faith,

Galatians 6:10
As we have therefore opportunity, let us do good unto all men, especially unto them who are of the household of faith.

Ephesians 1:15
Wherefore I also, after I heard of your faith in the Lord Jesus, and love unto all the saints,

Ephesians 2:8
For by grace are ye saved through faith; and that not of yourselves: it is the gift of God:

Ephesians 3:12
In whom we have boldness and access with confidence by the faith of him.

Ephesians 3:17
That Christ may dwell in your hearts by faith; that ye, being rooted and grounded in love,

Ephesians 4:5
One Lord, one faith, one baptism,

Ephesians 4:13
Till we all come in the unity of the faith, and of the knowledge of the Son of God, unto a perfect man, unto the measure of the stature of the fulness of Christ:

Ephesians 6:16
Above all, taking the shield of faith, wherewith ye shall be able to quench all the fiery darts of the wicked.

Ephesians 6:23
Peace be to the brethren, and love with faith, from God the Father and the Lord Jesus Christ.

Philippians 1:25
And having this confidence, I know that I shall abide and continue with you all for your furtherance and joy of faith;

Philippians 1:27
Only let your conversation be as it becometh the gospel of Christ: that whether I come and see you, or else be absent, I may hear of your affairs, that ye stand fast in one spirit, with one mind striving together for the faith of the gospel;

Philippians 2:17
Yea, and if I be offered upon the sacrifice and service of your faith, I joy, and rejoice with you all.

Philippians 3:9
And be found in him, not having mine own righteousness, which is of the law, but that which is through the faith of Christ, the righteousness which is of God by faith:

Colossians 1:2
To the saints and faithful brethren in Christ which are at Colosse: Grace be unto you, and peace, from God our Father and the Lord Jesus Christ.

Colossians 1:23
If ye continue in the faith grounded and settled, and be not moved away from the hope of the gospel, which ye have heard, and which was preached to every creature which is under heaven; whereof I Paul am made a minister;

Colossians 2:5
For though I be absent in the flesh, yet am I with you in the spirit, joying and beholding your order, and the stedfastness of your faith in Christ.

Colossians 2:7
Rooted and built up in him, and stablished in the faith, as ye have been taught, abounding therein with thanksgiving.

Colossians 2:12
Buried with him in baptism, wherein also ye are risen with him through the faith of the operation of God, who hath raised him from the dead.

1 Thessalonians 3:2
And sent Timotheus, our brother, and minister of God, and our fellow labourer in the gospel of Christ, to establish you, and to comfort you concerning your faith:

1 Thessalonians 3:5
For this cause, when I could no longer forbear, I sent to know your faith, lest by some means the tempter have tempted you, and our labour be in vain.

1 Thessalonians 5:8
But let us, who are of the day, be sober, putting on the breastplate of faith and love; and for an helmet, the hope of salvation.

1 Thessalonians 5:24
Faithful is he that calleth you, who also will do it.

2 Thessalonians 1:3
We are bound to thank God always for you, brethren, as it is meet, because that your faith groweth exceedingly, and the charity of every one of you all toward each other aboundeth;

2 Thessalonians 1:4
So that we ourselves glory in you in the churches of God for your patience and faith in all your persecutions and tribulations that ye endure:

2 Thessalonians 1:11
Wherefore also we pray always for you, that our God would count you worthy of this calling, and fulfil all the good pleasure of his goodness, and the work of faith with power:

2 Thessalonians 3:2
And that we may be delivered from unreasonable and wicked men: for all men have not faith.

2 Thessalonians 3:3
But the Lord is faithful, who shall stablish you, and keep you from evil.

1 Timothy 1:4
Neither give heed to fables and endless genealogies, which minister questions, rather than godly edifying which is in faith: so do.

1 Timothy 1:5
Now the end of the commandment is charity out of a pure heart, and of a good conscience, and of faith unfeigned:

1 Timothy 1:12
And I thank Christ Jesus our Lord, who hath enabled me, for that he counted me faithful, putting me into the ministry;

1 Timothy 1:19
Holding faith, and a good conscience; which some having put away concerning faith have made shipwreck:

1 Timothy 3:9
Holding the mystery of the faith in a pure conscience.

1 Timothy 3:11
Even so must their wives be grave, not slanderers, sober, faithful in all things.

1 Timothy 4:6
If thou put the brethren in remembrance of these things, thou shalt be a good minister of Jesus Christ, nourished up in the words of faith and of good doctrine, whereunto thou hast attained.

1 Timothy 4:12
Let no man despise thy youth; but be thou an example of the believers, in word, in conversation, in charity, in spirit, in faith, in purity.

1 Timothy 5:12
Having damnation, because they have cast off their first faith.

1 Timothy 6:11
But thou, O man of God, flee these things; and follow after righteousness, godliness, faith, love, patience, meekness.

1 Timothy 6:12
Fight the good fight of faith, lay hold on eternal life, whereunto thou art also called, and hast professed a good profession before many witnesses.

2 Timothy 1:13
Hold fast the form of sound words, which thou hast heard of me, in faith and love which is in Christ Jesus.

2 Timothy 2:2
And the things that thou hast heard of me among many witnesses, the same commit thou to faithful men, who shall be able to teach others also.

2 Timothy 2:11
It is a faithful saying: For if we be dead with him, we shall also live with him:

2 Timothy 2:13
If we believe not, yet he abideth faithful: he cannot deny himself.

2 Timothy 2:18
Who concerning the truth have erred, saying that the resurrection is past already; and overthrow the faith of some.

2 Timothy 2:22
Flee also youthful lusts: but follow righteousness, faith, charity, peace, with them that call on the Lord out of a pure heart.

2 Timothy 3:10
But thou hast fully known my doctrine, manner of life, purpose, faith, longsuffering, charity, patience,

2 Timothy 3:15
And that from a child thou hast known the holy scriptures, which are able to make thee wise unto salvation through faith which is in Christ Jesus.

2 Timothy 4:7
I have fought a good fight, I have finished my course, I have kept the faith:

Titus 1:9
Holding fast the faithful word as he hath been taught, that he may be able by sound doctrine both to exhort and to convince the gainsayers.

Titus 3:8
This is a faithful saying, and these things I will that thou affirm constantly, that they which have believed in God might be careful to maintain good works. These things are good and profitable unto men.

Titus 3:15
All that are with me salute thee. Greet them that love us in the faith. Grace be with you all. Amen.

Philemon 1:5
Hearing of thy love and faith, which thou hast toward the Lord Jesus, and toward all saints;

Philemon 1:6
That the communication of thy faith may become effectual by the acknowledging of every good thing which is in you in Christ Jesus.

Hebrews 2:17
Wherefore in all things it behoved him to be made like unto his brethren, that he might be a merciful and faithful high priest in things pertaining to God, to make reconciliation for the sins of the people.

Hebrews 3:2
Who was faithful to him that appointed him, as also Moses was faithful in all his house.

Hebrews 4:2
For unto us was the gospel preached, as well as unto them: but the word preached did not profit them, not being mixed with faith in them that heard it.

Hebrews 6:1
Therefore leaving the principles of the doctrine of Christ, let us go on unto perfection; not laying again the foundation of repentance from dead works, and of faith toward God,

Hebrews 6:12
That ye be not slothful, but followers of them who through faith and patience inherit the promises.

Hebrews 10:22
Let us draw near with a true heart in full assurance of faith, having our hearts sprinkled from an evil conscience, and our bodies washed with pure water.

Hebrews 10:23
Let us hold fast the profession of our faith without wavering; (for he is faithful that promised;)

Hebrews 10:38
Now the just shall live by faith: but if any man draw back, my soul shall have no pleasure in him.

Hebrews 11:1
Now faith is the substance of things hoped for, the evidence of things not seen.

Hebrews 11:3
Through faith we understand that the worlds were framed by the word of God, so that things which are seen were not made of things which do appear.

Hebrews 11:6
But without faith it is impossible to please him: for he that cometh to God must believe that he is, and that he is a rewarder of them that diligently seek him.

Hebrews 11:8
By faith Abraham, when he was called to go out into a place which he should after receive for an inheritance, obeyed; and he went out, not knowing whither he went.

Hebrews 11:9
By faith he sojourned in the land of promise, as in a strange country, dwelling in tabernacles with Isaac and Jacob, the heirs with him of the same promise:

Hebrews 11:11
Through faith also Sara herself received strength to conceive seed, and was delivered of a child when she was past age, because she judged him faithful who had promised.

Hebrews 11:13
These all died in faith, not having received the promises, but having seen them afar off, and were persuaded of them, and embraced them, and confessed that they were strangers and pilgrims on the earth.

Hebrews 11:17
By faith Abraham, when he was tried, offered up Isaac: and he that had received the promises offered up his only begotten son,

Hebrews 11:20
By faith Isaac blessed Jacob and Esau concerning things to come.

Hebrews 11:21
By faith Jacob, when he was a dying, blessed both the sons of Joseph; and worshipped, leaning upon the top of his staff.

Hebrews 11:22
By faith Joseph, when he died, made mention of the departing of the children of Israel; and gave commandment concerning his bones.

Hebrews 11:23
By faith Moses, when he was born, was hid three months of his parents, because they saw he was a proper child; and they were not afraid of the king's commandment.

Hebrews 11:24
By faith Moses, when he was come to years, refused to be called the son of Pharaoh's daughter;

Hebrews 11:27
By faith he forsook Egypt, not fearing the wrath of the king: for he endured, as seeing him who is invisible.

Hebrews 11:28
Through faith he kept the passover, and the sprinkling of blood, lest he that destroyed the firstborn should touch them.

Hebrews 11:29
By faith they passed through the Red sea as by dry land: which the Egyptians assaying to do were drowned.

Hebrews 11:33
Who through faith subdued kingdoms, wrought righteousness, obtained promises, stopped the mouths of lions.

Hebrews 11:39
And these all, having obtained a good report through faith, received not the promise:

Hebrews 12:2
Looking unto Jesus the author and finisher of our faith; who for the joy that was set before him endured the cross, despising the shame, and is set down at the right hand of the throne of God.

Hebrews 13:7
Remember them which have the rule over you, who have spoken unto you the word of God: whose faith follow, considering the end of their conversation.

James 1:3
Knowing this, that the trying of your faith worketh patience.

James 1:6
But let him ask in faith, nothing wavering. For he that wavereth is like a wave of the sea driven with the wind and tossed.

James 2:1
My brethren, have not the faith of our Lord Jesus Christ, the Lord of glory, with respect of persons.

James 2:5
Hearken, my beloved brethren, Hath not God chosen the poor of this world rich in faith, and heirs of the kingdom which he hath promised to them that love him?

James 2:14
What doth it profit, my brethren, though a man say he hath faith, and have not works? can faith save him?

James 2:17
Even so faith, if it hath not works, is dead, being alone.

James 2:18
Yea, a man may say, Thou hast faith, and I have works: shew me thy faith without thy works, and I will shew thee my faith by my works.

James 2:20
But wilt thou know, O vain man, that faith without works is dead?

James 2:22
Seest thou how faith wrought with his works, and by works was faith made perfect?

James 2:24
Ye see then how that by works a man is justified, and not by faith only.

James 2:26
For as the body without the spirit is dead, so faith without works is dead also.

James 5:15
And the prayer of faith shall save the sick, and the Lord shall raise him up; and if he have committed sins, they shall be forgiven him.

1 Peter 1:5
Who are kept by the power of God through faith unto salvation ready to be revealed in the last time.

1 Peter 1:7
That the trial of your faith, being much more precious than of gold that perisheth, though it be tried with fire, might be found unto praise and honour and glory at the appearing of Jesus Christ:

1 Peter 1:9
Receiving the end of your faith, even the salvation of your souls.

1 Peter 1:21
Who by him do believe in God, that raised him up from the dead, and gave him glory; that your faith and hope might be in God.

1 Peter 5:9
Whom resist stedfast in the faith, knowing that the same afflictions are accomplished in your brethren that are in the world.

2 Peter 1:1
Simon Peter, a servant and an apostle of Jesus Christ, to them that have obtained like precious faith with us through the righteousness of God and our Saviour Jesus Christ:

2 Peter 1:5
And beside this, giving all diligence, add to your faith virtue; and to virtue knowledge;

1 John 1:9
If we confess our sins, he is faithful and just to forgive us our sins, and to cleanse us from all unrighteousness.

1 John 5:4
For whatsoever is born of God overcometh the world: and this is the victory that overcometh the world, even our faith.

3 John 1:5
Beloved, thou doest faithfully whatsoever thou doest to the brethren, and to strangers;

Jude 1:3
Beloved, when I gave all diligence to write unto you of the common salvation, it was needful for me to write unto you, and exhort you that ye should earnestly contend for the faith which was once delivered unto the saints.

Jude 1:20
But ye, beloved, building up yourselves on your most holy faith, praying in the Holy Ghost,

PROTECTION

Psalm 91
He that dwelleth in the secret place of the most High shall abide under the shadow of the Almighty. I will say of the Lord, He is my refuge and my fortress: my God; in him will I trust. Surely he shall deliver thee from the snare of the fowler, and from the noisome pestilence. ...

Deuteronomy 32:38
Which did eat the fat of their sacrifices, and drank the wine of their drink offerings? let them rise up and help you, and be your protection.

Psalm 34: 7 GOD's angel sets up a circle
of protection around us while we pray. Message Translation

Psalm 91: 4 He shall cover you with His feathers,
and under His wings you shall find protection; MEV version

Psalm 17: 8 Keep me as the apple of Your eye;
hide me under the shadow of Your wings,

2 Thessalonians 3:3
3 But the Lord is faithful, and he will strengthen you and protect you from the evil one.

Psalm 57: 1 Have mercy on me, my God, have mercy on me, for in you I take refuge. I will take refuge in the shadow of your wings until the disaster has passed.

2222222222222222222

JOY

Galatians 5:22
But the fruit of the Spirit is love, joy, peace, longsuffering, gentleness, goodness, faith,

Nehemiah 8:10
Then he said unto them, Go your way, eat the fat, and drink the sweet, and send portions unto them for whom nothing is prepared: for this day is holy unto our Lord: neither be ye sorry; for the joy of the Lord is your strength.

Psalm 5:11
But let all those that put their trust in thee rejoice: let them ever shout for joy, because thou defendest them: let them also that love thy name be joyful in thee.

Psalm 16:11
Thou wilt shew me the path of life: in thy presence is fulness of joy; at thy right hand there are pleasures for evermore.

Psalm 21:1
The king shall joy in thy strength, O Lord; and in thy salvation how greatly shall he rejoice!

Psalm 27:6
And now shall mine head be lifted up above mine enemies round about me: therefore will I offer in his tabernacle sacrifices of joy; I will sing, yea, I will sing praises unto the Lord.

Psalm 30:5
For his anger endureth but a moment; in his favour is life: weeping may endure for a night, but joy cometh in the morning.

Psalm 32:11
Be glad in the Lord, and rejoice, ye righteous: and shout for joy, all ye that are upright in heart.

Psalm 35:9
And my soul shall be joyful in the Lord: it shall rejoice in his salvation.

Psalm 35:27
Let them shout for joy, and be glad, that favour my righteous cause: yea, let them say continually, Let the Lord be magnified, which hath pleasure in the prosperity of his servant.

Psalm 42:4
When I remember these things, I pour out my soul in me: for I had gone with the multitude, I went with them to the house of God, with the voice of joy and praise, with a multitude that kept holyday.

Psalm 43:4
Then will I go unto the altar of God, unto God my exceeding joy: yea, upon the harp will I praise thee, O God my God.

Psalm 48:2
Beautiful for situation, the joy of the whole earth, is mount Zion, on the sides of the north, the city of the great King.

Psalm 51:8
Make me to hear joy and gladness; that the bones which thou hast broken may rejoice.

Psalm 51:12
Restore unto me the joy of thy salvation; and uphold me with thy free spirit.

Psalm 63:5
My soul shall be satisfied as with marrow and fatness; and my mouth shall praise thee with joyful lips:

Psalm 65:13
The pastures are clothed with flocks; the valleys also are covered over with corn; they shout for joy, they also sing.

Psalm 66:1
Make a joyful noise unto God, all ye lands:

Psalm 67:4
O let the nations be glad and sing for joy: for thou shalt judge the people righteously, and govern the nations upon earth. Selah.

Psalm 81:1
Sing aloud unto God our strength: make a joyful noise unto the God of Jacob.

Psalm 89:15
Blessed is the people that know the joyful sound: they shall walk, O Lord, in the light of thy countenance.

Psalm 95:1
O come, let us sing unto the Lord: let us make a joyful noise to the rock of our salvation.

Psalm 95:2
Let us come before his presence with thanksgiving, and make a joyful noise unto him with psalms.

Psalm 96:12
Let the field be joyful, and all that is therein: then shall all the trees of the wood rejoice

Psalm 98:6
With trumpets and sound of cornet make a joyful noise before the Lord, the King.

Psalm 98:8
Let the floods clap their hands: let the hills be joyful together

Psalm 100:1
Make a joyful noise unto the Lord, all ye lands.

Psalm 105:43
And he brought forth his people with joy, and his chosen with gladness:

Psalm 113:9
He maketh the barren woman to keep house, and to be a joyful mother of children. Praise ye the Lord.

Psalm 126:5
They that sow in tears shall reap in joy.

Psalm 132:9
Let thy priests be clothed with righteousness; and let thy saints shout for joy.

Psalm 132:16
I will also clothe her priests with salvation: and her saints shall shout aloud
for joy.

Psalm 137:6
If I do not remember thee, let my tongue cleave to the roof of my mouth; if
I prefer not Jerusalem above my chief joy.

Psalm 149:2
Let Israel rejoice in him that made him: let the children of Zion be joyful in
their King.

Psalm 149:5
Let the saints be joyful in glory: let them sing aloud upon their beds.

Proverbs 12:20
Deceit is in the heart of them that imagine evil: but to the counsellors of
peace is joy.

Proverbs 14:10
The heart knoweth his own bitterness; and a stranger doth not intermeddle
with his joy.

Proverbs 15:21
Folly is joy to him that is destitute of wisdom: but a man of understanding
walketh uprightly.

Proverbs 15:23
A man hath joy by the answer of his mouth: and a word spoken in due
season, how good is it!

Proverbs 17:21
He that begetteth a fool doeth it to his sorrow: and the father of a fool hath
no joy.

Proverbs 21:15
It is joy to the just to do judgment: but destruction shall be to the workers
of iniquity.

Proverbs 23:24
The father of the righteous shall greatly rejoice: and he that begetteth a wise
child shall have joy of him.

FIGHTING

Genesis 12: 2 I will make of you a great nation;
  I will bless you
and make your name great,
  so that you will be a blessing.
3 I will bless them who bless you
  and curse him who curses you,[a]
and in you all families of the earth
  will be blessed."

2 Timothy 4:7
I have fought a good fight, I have finished my course, I have kept the faith:

Exodus 14:14
The Lord shall fight for you, and ye shall hold your peace.

Exodus 14:25
And took off their chariot wheels, that they drave them heavily: so that the Egyptians said, Let us flee from the face of Israel; for the Lord fighteth for them against the Egyptians.

Deuteronomy 1:30
The Lord your God which goeth before you, he shall fight for you, according to all that he did for you in Egypt before your eyes;

Deuteronomy 3:22
Ye shall not fear them: for the Lord your God he shall fight for you.

Deuteronomy 20:4
For the Lord your God is he that goeth with you, to fight for you against your enemies, to save you.

Joshua 23:10
One man of you shall chase a thousand: for the Lord your God, he it is that fighteth for you, as he hath promised you.

Psalm 144:1
Blessed be the Lord my strength which teacheth my hands to war, and my fingers to fight:

Jeremiah 1:19
And they shall fight against thee; but they shall not prevail against thee; for I am with thee, saith the Lord, to deliver thee.

1 Corinthians 9:26
I therefore so run, not as uncertainly; so fight I, not as one that beateth the air:

1 Timothy 6:12
Fight the good fight of faith, lay hold on eternal life, whereunto thou art also called, and hast professed a good profession before many witnesses.

2 Timothy 4:7
I have fought a good fight, I have finished my course, I have kept the faith:

OTHER BOOKS BY CHRIS LEGEBOW

Available on Amazon.ca Amazon.com or Kindle
Or the Create Space webstore.

Living Word Publishers

An Excellent Spirit: Living Life Wholly Unto God

Covenant With God: God's Relationship With Man

Discovering and Using your Spiritual Gifts

Encouraging Yourself in the Most Holy Faith

The Five-Fold Ministry: Gifts to the Church

Kinds of Prayer. Knowing Them and Using Them Effectively

Living Life Fully: Knowing your Purpose

The Anointing: the Glory of God

The High Calling: Life Worth Living

The Sacraments: A Charismatic Guide

ABOUT THE AUTHOR

Chris Legebow is a Christian Professor of English and Communications. She has taught at the elementary, high school and College and University levels. She has ministered in her local churches in intercessory prayer, teaching Sunday school and other Christian Doctrine classes to children and youths. She has preached to congregations and given her testimony. Although she was not raised in a Christian home, she came to know Jesus Christ as her Saviour and LORD while she was studying in University. This radically transformed her life in terms of priorities and commitment. She has a strong passion for the great commission – that Jesus Christ would be preached throughout all the earth believing that it a major sign of the LORD's return. She has been a part of several different types of full gospel charismatic churches but has also gained much of her insight and enlightenment from Christian Media and broadcasting. She hopes to continue ministering, serving, interceding and giving and teaching until the LORD returns.